Rewilding Prayer

Rewilding Prayer

God Beyond Gender, Faith Beyond Formulas

Sally Douglas

CASCADE *Books* • Eugene, Oregon

REWILDING PRAYER
God Beyond Gender, Faith Beyond Formulas

Copyright © 2025 Sally Douglas. All rights reserved. Liturgies may be utilized in worship, with full acknowledgement: Sally Douglas *Rewilding Prayer*. Cascade Books, 2025. Except for brief quotations in critical publications or reviews, no other part of this book may be reproduced in any manner without prior written permission from the publisher. Write: Permissions, Wipf and Stock Publishers, 199 W. 8th Ave., Suite 3, Eugene, OR 97401.

Cascade Books
An Imprint of Wipf and Stock Publishers
199 W. 8th Ave., Suite 3
Eugene, OR 97401

www.wipfandstock.com

PAPERBACK ISBN: 979-8-3852-4722-6
HARDCOVER ISBN: 979-8-3852-4723-3
EBOOK ISBN: 979-8-3852-4724-0

Cataloguing-in-Publication data:

Names: Douglas, Sally [author].

Title: Rewilding prayer : God beyond gender, faith beyond formulas / by Sally Douglas.

Description: Eugene, OR: Cascade Books, 2025 | Includes bibliographical references.

Identifiers: ISBN 979-8-3852-4722-6 (paperback) | ISBN 979-8-3852-4723-3 (hardcover) | ISBN 979-8-3852-4724-0 (ebook)

Subjects: LCSH: Prayers. | Prayer—Christianity. | Spiritual life—Christianity. | Spirituality. | Trinity. | Sexism in religion.

Classification: BV210 D66 2025 (paperback) | BV210 (ebook)

VERSION NUMBER 10/14/25

Scripture quotations marked (NRSV) are from the New Revised Standard Version Bible, copyright © 1989 the Division of Christian Education of the National Council of the Churches of Christ in the United States of America. Used by permission. All rights reserved.

For all who thirst for more (Psalm 42).

Contents

Acknowledgements | ix
List of Abbreviations | x

Part One: Prayer as the Call to the Real
1. Rewilding prayer | 3
2. Words and spaces | 12

Part Two: Praying in Daily Life
3. Pauses in the chaos | 31
4. Blessings in living and dying | 53
5. When there are no words | 68

Part Three: Praying in the Gathered Community
6. Joining the choirs of angels | 87
7. Beyond guilt trips | 122
8. Praying for others? | 145
9. This is my body | 166

Conclusion
10. Homeward Bound | 195

Bibliography | 203

Acknowledgements

I GIVE THANKS FOR DR. Jan Gray RSM who was fierce and encouraging when I began experimenting with fresh language for the Triune God. I am grateful for the people of Richmond Uniting Church, many of the liturgies in this book were composed during our ten years together. I am glad for my students, for colleagues, and for people across the UCA who continue to ask me to write. I am thankful for Robin Parry, an enthusiastic and clear-eyed editor. I am grateful to Andrew, my partner and friend, an attentive reader and staunch supporter. Jemimah and Zach, you are amazing, and we are so glad you are here. I am thankful for family and friends, for loud music, and for quiet retreats. I am grateful for those, both living and dead, who continue to teach me about prayer in their writing and practices. Finally to the Holy One–Sacred Three—my Author, my Anchor, my Advocate—all glory be to you. Thank you for the persistent call into life and freedom. May it be so.

List of Abbreviations

Gen	Genesis
2 Kgs	2 Kings
Ps	Psalms
Prov	Proverbs
Isa	Isaiah
Sir	Sirach
Bar	Baruch
Matt	Matthew
Rom	Romans
1 Cor	1 Corinthians
2 Cor	2 Corinthians
Gal	Galatians
Eph	Ephesians
Col	Colossians
Heb	Hebrews
Jas	James
1 Pet	1 Peter
Rev	Revelation
Did.	The Didache
1 Clem.	1 Clement
1 Apol.	Justin, *First Apology*
Dial.	Justin, *Dialogue with Trypho*
Apol.	Tertullian, *Apology*
Nat.	Tertullian, *To the Heathen*
NRSV	New Revised Standard Version

Part One
Prayer as the Call to the Real

1
Rewilding Prayer

WHEN YOU HEAR THE word "prayer" I wonder what images come to mind? In popular culture the dominant image of Christian prayer is of hands pressed together, fingers pointing skyward, and eyes looking pleadingly to heaven. In film, when characters pray often they are presented in one of two ways. Sometimes they are imaged as the (boring) faithful person, who mindlessly recites words in a cavernous church. Conversely, they are imaged as the unlikely pray-er, a hero who finds themselves in a desperate situation and as a last resort turns to prayer to bargain with some Zeus-like god who may, or may not, be listening and certainly cannot be trusted. While those among us who are Christians might feel a sense of frustration about the monotony of these depictions, we do not deserve the right to be outraged. This is because in many church communities our practices do little to disrupt these stereotypes.

Authentic prayer is a call to the real, not a deluded distraction from it. This book seeks to orient us to this reality, cutting through dominant assumptions to explore what it might mean to take our own experiences and a life of prayer seriously. Despite the popular imagery and the mechanistic patterns of praying in many churches, learning how to allow our truest selves (including our contradictions, giftedness, envy, insecurities, and clunkiness) to be open to the Source of all *is* the place in which profound transformation is finally able to happen. Things that seemed interminably bound up in our identity, weighing us down and sending us off course, are

PART ONE: PRAYER AS THE CALL TO THE REAL

able to be lifted. Insights, blind spots, childhood wounds, seething toxicity—in us or in others—all these things we studiously ignore in our busy, compulsed lives are able to break through to the surface and be met by One whose love is stronger than all our deathliness. Here the slow work of healing is able to begin.

Let me begin by sharing a story. Some years ago, I had a conversation with someone who told me that they used to pray but that this had changed. They explained to me that when they realized that they had not prayed for months, and more than that, had not missed praying during this period, they concluded that they were no longer a person of faith. Consequently they stepped away from the church. I am not sure how I responded at the time. However, over the years I have continued to ponder this conversation, wondering how many people feel the same way. How many of us find in adolescence, or at some point in adulthood, that praying feels empty? When people find that their experience of prayer becomes tedious, or lacks substance and grit, or has little transformative impact, how often do they assume that their faith must have dried up? Similarly, I wonder how often people think that they have failed at praying, or that there is no God, when their prayers are not answered—or not in a way that they can recognize. That fleeting conversation has served as something like a seed for this book.

The truth is that prayer is not like ascending on a heavenly escalator. We do not move from one great enlightenment moment to another. Instead, we muddle through, understanding and failing to understand, experiencing consolation and falling into despair, feeling empty, tasting joy, doubting, believing, and doubting, over and over again. This is part of the life of following Jesus. What is curious is that while these realities diverge from church rhetoric and the expectations we might foist upon ourselves, or one another, this is just how the first disciples are depicted across the Gospels—read Mark's Gospel right through to get the bluntest depiction of the disciples lunging from doubt, to fleeting insight, to doubt.

Across denominations in the church we regularly fail to resource people in their spiritual journeys (as well as in other ways). Within the context of prayer this falling short takes diverse forms. In many congregations, both high and low, contemporary or traditional, prayers appear to be recited or performed rather than prayed. In some churches the possibility of openness to the Most High is suffocated by language that pretends that God is a man. As we will explore, insistence upon addressing the Composer of all with only male pronouns limits God and denies the rich diversity of language and imagery within the biblical text. Indeed, this habit has become a form of idolatry in many places. As a consequence of this false devotion, vast swathes of the population cannot imagine that there is anything good in the news of Jesus, and women continue to be excluded and misused. Words matter.

In some churches, the desire to be accessible leads to worship being flattened out so much that the presence of the Divine is barely acknowledged. In such settings the scandalous distinctiveness of Christian faith dissolves into generic prayers that could, without too much difficulty, be readily used as gratitude prompts in a wellness retreat. In many worship services, across denominations, prayers of intercession appear to be driven by the assumption that the Source of all is not informed about the tragedies that have unfolded during the week, and it is the responsibility of the Christian to compile these for the Divine in a shopping list of doom. In most worship contexts, silence appears to be squeezed to the edges. Is it any wonder that prayer begins to feel empty?

It is true that there are worship leaders, both lay and ordained, who continue to deepen their relationship with the Divine as they explore, wrestle, and grow in their own prayer lives. It is also true that there are dynamic faith communities, large and small, seeking to pray together week by week with honesty, seriousness, and openness to the Most High. Thanks be to God. However, too often this is the exception to the rule. When people leave the church, saying that they are "spiritual not religious" I have empathy with them. While part of this decision may be informed by the legalism or hypocrisy within the institution, I suspect that this is also often driven by a deep hunger that is not being met in the church. If we are unable to create space for the real—for wild, wrestling, transforming abiding with the Living One—it is only natural that people will walk away. Some will leave to seek soul nourishment in other contexts that promise a different expression of spirituality. Others will come to the conclusion that such sustenance does not exist and shut down this part of themselves. We have much to confess and to turn away from across our churches.

The reasons why prayer has been made pietistic, boring, and empty in so many churches are complex. Habits shape expectations for how we should be. The unspoken view that "this is how we do worship" can smother the opportunity to raise concerns or dare to dream about how things could be done differently. Fashions can overtake (think PowerPoint or organs). Hierarchies can make it impossible to ask questions. For at least some within the worldwide household of Christian faith, I suspect there is a deep fear that there may be no God, or at least not a God who listens and acts. This problematizes prayer considerably. In contrast, at least for some, I imagine the opposite fear exists. If we dare to be authentically open to the Divine, rather than merely saying words *at* the Divine, it will be risky because we will be confronted with truth and grace. Reciting words is a far safer option.

Alongside these issues, I think there is another factor that contributes enormously to our current (non)practices of praying. It is commonly assumed by Christians that people know how to pray because prayer is understood to be *natural*. Children and young people might be taught a smattering of simple prayers. However, in many church contexts once people are adults the practice of prayer does not appear to be discussed. Instead, it is taken for granted that people have a shared understanding, not only of how to pray, but also of what prayer might be for, and what it might achieve. As a consequence, opportunities to explore these crucial and complex questions are often few and far between. Instead, we say prayers in church and encourage people to pray for others at home, leaving them to get on with this alone, even when their inner life feels like a heap of dry bones.

These issues are compounded by the reality that in many seminaries and faith-education contexts people are often given little space to wrestle with these questions out loud. Students are not given experiential access to the beautiful and vast array of prayer practices that are part of our Christian tradition. If emerging leaders are not able to ask the questions on their hearts, to name their unbelief, and to experiment with, be left cold by, upended through, and be nourished by a range of prayer practices, how will they be able to facilitate such conversations or share such treasures in the faith communities that they go on to serve?

While prayer may be natural, this does not make it easy. Walking is also natural for most people. This does not mean that it is simple to learn to walk. When toddlers learn this skill, they need time and an array of supports. First, they need to see people walking so that they can copy them. Then, they usually need things to pull themselves up on, or kind hands to steady them. Little ones need to strengthen their leg muscles and get used to using them in this new way, and they need to come to terms with the tricky issue of balance. It helps if they have encouragement, cheer leaders offering words of support and whoops of delight when they stand and begin to take their first steps. It also helps when they are offered tender comfort when they fall. Toddlers need time to practice, to fail, and to try again. As toddlers grows in their confidence to walk independently, they lose the need for these first supports. This does not mean that they are walking less faithfully. Instead, they are walking differently because they have grown. So it is with the process of learning to pray.

The things that support us to pray as a child, young person, or a person new to faith are invaluable. Like little ones learning to walk, as we learn to pray we will likely need clear and accessible resources and kind people to support us, encourage us, and pick us up when we fall. However, as we grow and develop, many of the first prayer styles we were introduced to may no longer offer nourishment. This is not because of a lack of faith on our part or a consequence of growing away from the Divine. Rather, this is because we are growing in maturity, even though it may not feel like

PART ONE: PRAYER AS THE CALL TO THE REAL

it at the time. Prayer styles that once gave our lives meaning may become empty because we are in a new stage of our life and faith journey, and we need different resources for the road before us.

When we travel through various experiences, we are called into different ways of being with the Divine that make sense in this new context. This is particularly the case when we are confronted with unexpected tragedy. In deep suffering, our crisp edges and naïve certainties are hacked away, and any rose-colored ideas of God and happy-ever-after constructions of faith are obliterated. In this desolate land—which may also be a gateway to liberation—we will need new words and ways of embodying prayer if we are to maintain our integrity and be open to the Divine. Thankfully we do not have to invent these ways of being on our own. Across the tradition there are resources and stories and wisdom from the diverse communion of saints to draw from and engage with. Instead of churches holding people back by continuing to offer simplistic patterns of prayer that help us to take our first steps, imagine if we engaged seriously together with these treasures. We may learn how to tell the truth and listen for the truth. We may learn how to walk. We may also learn how to run fast and even soar, and create space for others to do so as well.

Beyond the tropes of prayer as a mindless rote exercise or a desperate attempt at haggling, Christian prayer is about learning how to be in relationship, just as we are, with the fierce One who is love (John 15:4; 1 John 4:8–9; Rev 1:12–16). In my experience, entering into this abiding is a bit like choosing to stand very close to a fire. It is illuminating, energizing, and dangerous. Learning to speak in our rawness and to listen with attentiveness to the Source of all will change us. Here we will taste nourishment for our inner beings (John 4:14; 6:35). Here the eyes of our hearts will be opened (Eph 1:18; 1 Clem. 36:2). In such praying we will begin to recognize our own truths amidst the gritty realities of living and dying and we will be drawn into a larger story—the Divine's unfolding drama of grace. At times this can be amazing. We will be birthed into increasingly honest and compassionate relationships with the Beloved, with others, and with ourselves. This can also be annoying. And painful. In living close to the fire, our cosy illusions about life and God, and our cleverly disguised ego narratives, whether we prefer casting ourselves as the victim or the savior, will be exposed and slowly dissolved so that healing may begin to take place. It is the road to freedom, but it is not easy.

This book offers a weaving together of discussions about praying and a fresh collection of prayers, blessings, and liturgies for use in daily life and for use in worshipping communities. For ten years I worked in the mode of "scholar pastor," serving as the minister in an inner-city parish in Melbourne, Australia, while also lecturing, researching, and writing in the fields New Testament, early church studies, and theology. Over this time people have continued to ask if they may utilize my prayers and liturgies. *Rewilding Prayer* offers a sample of these, and others that I have composed. These resources seek to be faithful, expansive, and to stretch beyond the formulaic. However, they are not an end point in themselves. Instead the prayers and structures in this book seek to assist us in being ourselves and being attuned to the Blessed Three in whom "deep calls to deep" (Ps 42:7).[1]

Throughout this collection, the biblical text and theology are engaged with robustly, both in relation to questions about praying and in the choice of language within the prayers. The Triune God, the God of Christian faith, is at the center of worship in these resources. The language utilized may, at first, seem new or strange. Diverse Old Testament imagery, that moves beyond gendered language for God, is reclaimed. New Testament and early church proclamations of Jesus in the language and imagery of the female divine, Sophia, is retrieved.[2] Here we are encountered by the Most High, the Blessed Three: Holy Mystery, Holy Wisdom, Holy Flame. In reclaiming such naming for God, it is not being suggested that the dominant language of "Father, Son, and Holy Spirit" needs to

---

1. All biblical quotes from the New Revised Standard Version unless otherwise stated.

2. This early church understanding will be explored in chapter 2, for detailed discussion see Douglas, *Early Church Understandings of Jesus as the Female Divine*; Douglas, *Jesus Sophia*.

PART ONE: PRAYER AS THE CALL TO THE REAL

be excluded. This would be to replicate the kind of harm that has been enacted through the centuries.

The book is divided into three parts. In Part One, we explore questions of language, theology, the biblical text, and the gifts and risks of seeking to carve out time for prayer. In Part Two, prayers and blessings are offered for use in daily life, for a myriad of specific occasions. Throughout, prayer is discussed with raw honesty, and this section concludes with a chapter exploring what we might do when we cannot pray. In Part Three of the book, a collection of liturgies for church communities is offered. In these chapters, theological ideas and unspoken assumptions are examined, ancient understandings are retrieved, and fresh words are offered for prayers of adoration, letting go (confession), intercession, and Holy Communion. The final chapter of the book draws the threads together and offers one final liturgy for use at home.

While written prayers can be (and often are) empty, performative, or both, it is also true that structure is able to create freedom. In the absence of structures we can get lost in our heads, or the loudest and most powerful voices can dominate. Liturgies that follow the shape carved out by ancient patterns of communal prayer, that are grounded in the biblical text, and that attend to real life—liturgies that are prayerfully led and that include spaces for silence—can be sites of transformation. I know this from experience. While it may seem baffling in our technological age, liturgies have power. They can help us to tell the truth, particularly when we have no words, or are struggling to find them. Liturgies can assist us in navigating a way through life's joys and disasters, but not in a way that asks us to suspend our grief or play make believe. Instead, when liturgies are authentic and grounded in the risen, crucified One, they can be like a coracle in a storm, carrying us amidst the waves, to come barefaced before the Living One *as we are*, not as we think we should be.

In the *Basis of Union*, the foundation document of the Uniting Church in Australia, it is poignantly stated that the church "prays that it may be ready when occasion demands to confess the Lord in fresh words and deeds" (para. 11). *Rewilding Prayer* seeks to contribute something to this endeavor, offering a sample of how we might pray with guts and integrity amidst the chaos. You may like to dip in and out of chapters as you need them. You may like to read straight through. You may like to read with others. In turn, you may be inspired to write your own prayers and blessings. In whatever ways you use this book, I hope that it may be useful for telling the truth and gathering to the real. The ferocious compassion of the Living One awaits.

2
Words and spaces

THIS IS NOT A chapter that outlines the five easy rules for how and when you should pray. Nor are the words of the prayers that are offered in the chapters that follow intended to be prescriptive. How could this be the case? As traced in chapter 1, at different seasons in our lives, at different spaces in our faith-and-doubt journey, the ways in which we will pray meaningfully will vary enormously. At heart, prayer in Christian tradition is not about reciting particular words, striving for best practice, or praying out of habit, guilt, or in the flaccid hope of gaining divine favor. Instead, praying is about learning how to abide with, dwell with, *be* with the Living One who is beyond our imagining. This is a journey of a lifetime. It will change, and it will change us.

At the outset I need to underscore the risk. The experience of abiding with the Divine is not an invitation into a sunset-tinged state of bliss. This is not a relationship in which we will be constantly affirmed or consoled, nor is the spiritual life a competition. Christian discipleship is not a linear progression from one revelation to another as we reach ever higher plains. Instead, it is a rugged process of dying and rising over and over. Along the way there will be epiphanies and devastations, desert temptings, and sabbath rests, feasts and fasts, learning and unlearning, loneliness, unexpected community, growth, and pruning. Seeking to abide within the Divine is dangerous. This is because we will be called to face ugly truths. We will be challenged to recognize our wounds and our weapons, and those of others, and to put down our myriad charades. We will begin to listen to our pain and attend to our brokenness. And we will slowly be enabled to look at others with eyes of grace. We will be challenged out of the stories we love to endlessly tell ourselves, so that we may enter the vastness of possibility. We will be relentlessly called to allow the Holy One to haul us into healing so that we may be truly restored and re-storied.[1] In vital, confronting relationship with the Divine, life is not static or comfortable. We will find ourselves invited to dwell more and more deeply in truth and compassion, for ourselves and for others.

Abiding in the Divine is hard, brave work. However, this is always a choice. Across the Gospel narratives, we discover that Jesus never forces anyone to follow. The invitation to "come and see" (John 1:39) is endlessly made and the choice to walk away is always available (see John 6:66). The image of Jesus in the dreamscape text of Revelation evokes this with beauty. Here Jesus says:

> Listen! I am standing at the door, knocking; if you hear my voice and open the door, I will come in to you and eat with you, and you with me. (Rev 3:20)

William Holman Hunt, an artist painting in the late 1800s and early 1900s, made a painting of this entitled "The Light of the World." In order to complete the work, he travelled to the Holy Land to study the light and architecture, over years he went on to paint different versions of this image. In 1904 one of these paintings went on a world tour. Can you imagine? Millions of people around the globe lined up to gaze upon this artwork. When "The Light of the World" came to Australia it is estimated that 80 percent of the population went to see it. More than a century on, whether we appreciate the artistic style or not, Jesus' invitation continues to shimmer. The Holy Human One is waiting at the door knocking. This is the One who continues to ask, "Do you want to be made well?" (John 5:6) and each day we choose how we will respond.

---

1. For use of the language of "re-storied," see Henderson-Espinoza, *Activist Theology*.

PART ONE: PRAYER AS THE CALL TO THE REAL

Despite the tender invitation, we often seek to avoid contact with the Source of all by keeping the door of our messy hearts firmly closed. This occurs beyond the church certainly, but this also occurs within Christian communities. Some avoid the Divine through addiction, whether to social media or other drugs. While less obvious, many avoid the presence of God by being busy. Doing good works and fighting for justice can be excellent ways to gain social approval *while* judiciously avoiding contact with the Source of all. The possibility that there might be life-changing consequences if we are open to the Divine leads many of us to prefer our addictions and habits of talking *at* God, rather than actually attending to the Divine's presence in the now. Indeed, it seems many Christians live out a kind of practical atheism in which theological ideas are talked about, just as atheists discuss such theories, but day-to-day life is bereft of meaningful relationship with the Divine.

In healthy, nourishing relationships, whether these be friendships or romantic relationships, there is reciprocity. There is both speaking and listening. In such relationships the texture of the listening is marked by attending, rather than waiting for our turn to speak, and through this both are changed. Beyond the dominant images of God as an all-controlling Zeus figure, beyond the common imagery of God as an unpredictable Santa, a bearded old man on a cloud from whom "we better watch out," beyond our silent fears that God is dead, the Source of all, the Triune God, is present, moving, uncontainable, *and* attentive. If we are raw and learn to shut up, the Divine who dwells with us in Jesus will listen to us and speak. The Holy One–Sacred Three will disrupt us, tell us to get up, turn over our tables, and bring life out of death within us and within our communities. The prayers and practices throughout these chapters are not magic solutions that solve the "problem" of praying. They are, instead, offered as examples of how we might be honest and how we might listen. At the outset there are three things to highlight about the texture of these prayers, blessings, and liturgies.

God beyond gender

In Christian tradition the prayers that have most often been preserved and handed down through the centuries refer to the Most High in male language. To pretend that the Composer of this vast universe is a man or must only be referred to in male language is absurd. In light of the richness of the imagery for God within the biblical text, this dogged idolatry is incongruous. Throughout the Bible we see diverse language and imagery for God. I have written extensively about this elsewhere, here we will trace this evidence briefly, so that you may gain a taste. Within the Psalms, the ancient book of prayer, sacred for both Jewish and Christian people, myriad metaphors for God are utilized. Here, for example, God is a rock (Ps 18:2) and the Most High (Ps 56:2); God is a bird (Ps 57:1); God is a refuge and stronghold (Ps 144:2); God is a mother who holds us on her lap (Ps 131:1–2). The ancient composers of the Psalms knew that the vastness of God could not be contained by one set of words, one image, or by one gender. Why have we forgotten this? When did we become shy about proclaiming this truth?

Alongside the Psalms, the reality that God is not male is also made plain in the first creation story (Gen 1:1—2:3). Here in the biblical text it is proclaimed that God utters creation into being and declares all things to be good. In the opening pages of the Bible, with clarity and precision, it is stated that God makes men and women *equally in God's image* (Gen 1:27). Here, and this needs to be underscored, women reflect God's image, just as men do. In this first creation story, ontological equality between the genders is proclaimed. Our language for God must therefore reflect this. In Genesis 2 a different emphasis within the theology of the human person is present. While not all scholars interpret this account in a hierarchical way, for those wishing to assert male domination, including within the Godhead, the second creation story has been a convenient text, utilized in order to justify the exclusion and silencing of women.[2] However, if we are to treat the biblical text

---

2. For further discussion of the use of the first and second creation stories in Christian tradition, see Douglas, "Jesus' Impact on Understandings of Gender," 155–78.

PART ONE: PRAYER AS THE CALL TO THE REAL

with integrity we need to honor its complexity and read each of these creation stories, written by different communities for different theological purposes, on their own terms.

There is more within the biblical text that underscores that faithful language for God does not need to be male. Within the earliest church, as people sought to give voice to their astonishing conviction that in Jesus God had graced humanity in person, Jesus communities turned to female divine imagery to proclaim this. Again and again within the New Testament, Jesus is imaged as Woman Wisdom—Sophia, the Wisdom of God. This female divine figure (*Sophia* in Greek; *Hokmah* in Hebrew) is found in the Old Testament. Here, she is with God before creation, infusing all things and offering her feast to all. She is integral to the Book of Proverbs (see Prov 8:1—9:6 for an introduction), as well as to Sirach, Baruch, and the Wisdom of Solomon. Jesus is imaged as Sophia within the Gospel of Matthew and in the Gospel of John. What is more, before the Gospels were composed, and even before some of Paul's letters were written, diverse Jesus communities were worshipping Jesus in the language and imagery of the female divine, Woman Wisdom. We see this evidence in the early hymn fragments that are preserved in the New Testament. These include the Colossians hymn (Col 1:15-20), the Hebrews hymn (Heb 1:2-4), the hymn fragment found in Paul's letter to Corinth (1 Cor 8:6; see also 1 Cor 1:24, 30), and the Johannine prologue (John 1:1-18).[3]

The biblical warrant for using male and female language for God is clear. So too is the invitation to utilize non-gendered imagery for the Divine as the composers of the Psalms do when they use the language of water, rock, or refuge. Despite the male pronouns that dominate our prayers, art, and worship songs, the Source of all is more vast than all of our limited language and conceptions, including those of gender. Glib insistence upon only addressing God as man is an insult to the biblical text and to the expansiveness of the Divine. It is also lazy. This strongly guarded

---

3. To explore this evidence in detail, see Douglas, *Jesus Sophia*, 10-49; Douglas, *Early Church Understandings of Jesus as the Female Divine*, 15-69.

habit is an affront to people of all genders and to the majority of Christian church attendees: women. Insistence upon pretending that God is a man, consciously and subconsciously, has served as a convenient tool for denying the God-given power and authority of women in the church and the world, with tragic, and often violent, consequences. In the prayers and liturgies in this book you will notice an absence of gendered language for God. Instead, the prayers are informed by the rich biblical imagery that is offered to us all, and that has been overlooked for so long.

The Blessed Three

The second thing to highlight is that again and again I seek to address God as the Blessed Three. When I was a candidate for ordained ministry, I studied at an extraordinary institution called the United Faculty of Theology. It was a theological college made up of academics from the Society of Jesus (the Jesuits), the Uniting Church in Australia (formed in the 1970s through a union of the Methodist, Presbyterian, and Congregational denominations), and the Anglican tradition. Teachers from these diverse denominations worked together, with classes made up of ordinand students and private students from each of these traditions and beyond. I studied "The Triune God" with the systematic theologian Dr. Jan Gray, RSM. It was extraordinary to wrestle with ideas of the Trinity with this gifted teacher and Sister of Mercy. She introduced us to a variety of thinkers, beginning with the biblical text. She began each class with a reflection on an artwork, and wove music into each lesson (including the song "American Pie"). Towards the end of the course, after tracing trinitarian understandings from the earliest church to our contemporary context, Jan challenged us about prayer. She said something to this effect: "If you are not worshipping God as Three and as One, you are not actually praying to the God of Christian faith." I was disrupted and inspired.

For Christians, in church and within our daily lives, where do our convictions about the Triune God show up? How often do we pray to the Blessed Three in worship, at home, at work, or in the

PART ONE: PRAYER AS THE CALL TO THE REAL

car? It seems that many people in the church, secretly and not so secretly, find the idea of God being Three and yet One confusing, embarrassing, or irrelevant. How would you even begin to explain this theology to someone unfamiliar with Christian faith? As a result, this theology is often ignored, and prayers are addressed to a nondescript "God." One of the many consequences of this habit is that the "God" envisioned continues to be an amalgam of Zeus, Santa, and any number of childhood constructions or Renaissance artworks depicting the Divine.

Alongside the complexity of thinking about God as Three and as One, there is another significant block that precludes people from drawing near to the idea of the Triune God. For many the idea of the Blessed Three is utterly alienating because of the language used in those churches that do retain a focus on the Trinity. The formulation "Father, Son, and Holy Spirit" is utterly alienating for many. While it is the case that the language of Father and Son is not about the gender of God, but rather denotes the relationship and self-giving identity within the Godhead, this imagery has provided ample textual warrant for the denial of the legitimacy of women priests, women leaders, and indeed, of women as fully autonomous people. In light of this perpetual violence, discomfit with the maleness of this language for the Triune God is justified.

For New Testament writers, however, the purpose of this language is very different. The language of Father and Son is not about divine anatomy. Nor is this language originally utilized in order to subjugate women. Instead this imagery is utilized by early communities as they seek to point to their wild convictions about the shared essence and intimate relationship between the Most High and the One who dwells with us in person in Jesus. Metaphor is being employed to give expression to this wondrous claim. This reality is made explicit in the Johannine prologue in which it is stated: "we have seen his glory, *as of* a father's only son" (John 1:14). The metaphorical nature of this language is underscored again in this passage, as the Son is described as being "close to the Father's *breast*" (John 1:18).[4]

---

4. Many English translations, including the NRSV, recoil from this

WORDS AND SPACES

The metaphorical imagery of Father and Son is one way that early writers attempt to give expression to the extraordinary conviction that the Holy One has fully come among us in person in Jesus. At the beginning of John's prologue different metaphorical imagery is used to give expression to this same conviction. Here, relying on Wisdom Christology, the author chooses to focus on the language of the Word: "the Word was with God and was God" (John 1:1).[5] Recognizing that all language for God within the biblical text, including Father and Son language, is metaphorical—always pointing towards the great mystery of divine being—is essential for mature Christian faith.

Within prayer and theology the language that is used can draw us into intimacy with the Divine, or it can repel us. For those beyond the church, the language we use can bar entry, stymieing the possibility of even exploring whether Christian faith may have something to offer. While some find comfort in the language of Father, Son, and Holy Spirit, it is heartbreaking that the beauty of trinitarian theology is obscured for so many by insistence upon the dominance of this one construction of words to the virtual exclusion of others. It does not need to be this way. It was in Jan's class that I began to seriously experiment with new language for the Blessed Three, working to retrieve ancient biblical imagery and making fresh words for prayer. I am grateful to Jan for her firm and encouraging response to these first faltering steps.

In light of the ambiguity towards trinitarian theology in many places, let me say a little more about why this theology is a gift to be reclaimed. While some argue that there is no evidence of the Trinity in the New Testament, this is not the case. What is not in the New Testament is a clearly stepped out doctrine of the Triune God. To be fair, most Christian doctrines are not stepped out in detail in the biblical text. Within the New Testament what is present, again and again, are convictions about the Blessed Three. We see this, for example, in the blessing that Paul quotes at the end

---

destabilizing imagery of the Father, and choose to mistranslate the Greek *kolpon*, which means breast or bosom, into the word heart.

5. See Douglas, *Early Church Understandings*, 47–48.

of his second letter to the people in Corinth, a blessing that is still used today: "The grace of the Lord Jesus Christ, the love of God, and the communion of the Holy Spirit be with all of you" (2 Cor 13:13). Within this blessing we see the experiential texture of this understanding. Something is happening in the lives of Jesus communities that is to do with grace, love, and fellowship and they are experiencing this through the Persons of the Blessed Three. What is more, this ancient blessing indicates that it is expected that these experiences of divine intimacy and love will continue.

We also discover the centrality of experience when Paul speaks about prayer in Romans. Here Paul reflects on the power of the Triune God within the shared lives of Jesus communities. He claims that through the power of the Spirit there is new adoption. People who are rich and poor, slaves and free Roman citizens are now *all* children of God and they are empowered to cry out to God as "Abba" (Rom 8:15). This word is the Aramaic for father or dad.[6] Again, it must be underscored that this language is not about the gender of God. In contrast, Paul is audaciously asserting that all kinds of people are being caught up into intimate relationship with the Divine, through the power of the Spirit *as* they discover that they are now co-heirs with Christ (Rom 8:15–17). Experience of the Triune God undergirds these proclamations.

Due to the saturation of Father language in the church it may be hard for us to hear the magnitude of what is being claimed by Paul. In the Greco-Roman world in which emperors such as Augustus were asserting that they were the son of god, in which slaves were seen as property rather than as human, and women were seen as incomplete men, to proclaim that low-status people—including slaves, women, and foreigners—were children of God was shocking. Yet Paul makes this claim based on the ongoing experiences of the Blessed Three across Jesus communities.

---

6. The naming of God as Abba almost definitely goes back to remembered teachings and experiences of Jesus. This term is cherished in different Jesus communities, as reflected in the evidence of the Aramaic being preserved within the Greek of New Testament texts (see Rom 8:15; Gal 4:6). Notably, in Mark's Gospel, in the midst of Jesus' agony in the garden on the night of betrayal, this language is preserved in Jesus' cry (Mark 14:36).

We also see the significance of spiritual experience in the early development of understandings of God as Three and yet One in Ephesians. Within this letter, liturgies and blessings abound. These prayers may have been part of the worshipping life of various Jesus communities in the earliest church. In one of these prayers we see the plumbline between convictions about the Blessed Three *and* the ongoing place of transformative encounter with the Divine. The author states:

> For this reason I bow my knees before the *Father*, from whom every family in heaven and on earth takes it name. I pray that, according to the riches of his glory, he may grant that you may be *strengthened in your inner being* with power through his *Spirit*, and that *Christ* may dwell in your hearts through faith, as you are being rooted and grounded in love. (Eph 3:14–17)

It is worth reading this whole passage slowly, and repeatedly.

Across this early evidence, likely penned before the oft-cited trinitarian words in Matthew's "great commission" (Matt 28:20), these texts point toward experiences of the Triune God. These authors are not trying to convince people about a confusing doctrine. To be fair trinitarian understandings must have been confusing to both Jewish people committed to monotheism and Greco-Roman people who worshipped a plethora of gods and goddesses. These first authors and communities are, instead, speaking about the *felt power* of the *Holy Spirit* drawing them into ever deepening relationship with the *Word made flesh* who has lived among them in fierce compassion, who is killed by the state, and who is raised, and with the *Source of all*. To put this plainly, these unexpected experiences of the Triune God changed the texture of their lives so much so that they had no other choice but to tell about it in this strange new way.

To take seriously the claim that God is in community within God's own self *does not* demand that we use only one set of words to speak about this. However, to take this theology seriously *does* demand that those importunate images of God as a lonely king upon a cloud be dismantled. In drawing close to the Blessed

Trinity, images of God as a solo monarch are toppled. In wrestling with the conviction that, within God's self, God is Three and yet One, a community of love and reciprocity, is to have our empire-shaped thinking undone. In taking triune theology seriously the legitimacy of tyrannical hierarchies and the power of patriarchy are dissolved. The worldwide church still has much to learn about this—and to repent. Like those in the earliest church, when we turn with seriousness to the Holy One–Sacred Three we find ourselves encountered by the Divine Community, endlessly flowing in self-giving and receiving grace. Here we are confronted with the Divine Dance of Love, and we too will be changed.[7]

In trinitarian theology we are called to liberative restoration. This is because if in some serious (not literal) way we are made "in the image" of the Divine (Gen 1:26) and, within God's self, God is Three Persons and yet One, then there are profound implications for us. Here we are called to be *ourselves*, our own person, and at the same time we are called to be in life-giving *community*. This demands that we be set free from the pattern of dissolving our personality in order to gain the acceptance of others. Equally, this demands that we resist the temptation to flee from community and the vulnerability of friendship. Each of us will likely fall prey to one of these tendencies. We are called into communities of authenticity, reciprocity, and mutuality that reflect the Divine Life. As we are reoriented into the center—the costly, flowing, and generous life of God within God's self—we will find balance as we learn to love our actual, spiky selves and have boundaries, while also living kindly and generously towards others. By grace, as our lives

---

7. The word *perichōrēsis* (from the Greek word for rotation) has a sense of fluid movement about it and was first used by John of Damascus (675 CE–749 CE) to reflect on "the dynamic and vital character" of each of the persons of the Trinity. LaCugna, *God for Us*, 270. Subsequently, the image of the dance has been used to give expression to this idea within the being of God. As Catherine LaCugna states: "The image of the dance forbids us to think of God as solitary. The idea of trinitarian *perichōrēsis* provides a marvelous point of entry into contemplating what it means to say that God is alive from all eternity as love." La Cugna, *God for Us*, 272.

begin to mirror who and how the Divine is, we will begin to taste freedom and homecoming.

One final observation. The challenge to take the Triune God into our heart-lives does not preclude the possibility of addressing prayers to one person of the Trinity. There are times when we are stirred to pray to Mother Father God, or to God the Word made flesh in Jesus, or to God the Advocate, Holy Spirit. May we always resist extremes and learn to be comfortable with the reality that the truth often resides in paradoxes such as both/and.

Silence

The third thing to highlight is that time and again there will be invitations in the prayers, blessings, and liturgies to stop talking. For a book that contains so many words about praying and so many words for prayer, what I am about to say may sound strange. The underlying foundation of prayer is learning how to be quiet and open. This is because if we are to be in abiding relationship with the Divine we need to learn how to *attend* to the Divine. That is, we need to learn how to stop dominating the conversation. At least in my experience, this is an incredibly hard thing to do. Silence, especially in the company of others in worship, can feel very strange. In Western settings where collective silence is now so often excluded from daily life, this is particularly so. Silence can feel awkward. Stomachs rumble. Minds wander. Silence can feel like a trap, or an absence. It can be boring. Perhaps this is especially so now, because people are constantly stimulated by the dopamine hits of social media, and left with brains that crave more and more of this "junk food" to get through the day.

Silence can also be frightening. This is because all of the things that we work so hard to avoid in our lives will begin to come to the surface, often quite quickly. In learning to be still, the truth is able to be heard over the clamor. The broken friendship, the dying dream, the childhood trauma, the mean spiritedness at work, the insecurities, the rude words at home, all of these things will come up. I suspect this is why so many of us quickly reject a silent practice, saying that it is not for us. It is very hard—and takes a good deal of courage—to face the shadows within and around us and stay present. But this is the thing, when the wounds and the pain begin to speak this is not because we are called into a life of grovelling penance. The opposite is true. The Triune God longs to heal us and bring us into love and joy and peace (Gal 5:22). However, we cannot be made well while we are busy pretending that everything is fine.

Engaging with practices that help us to be quiet before the Holy One–Sacred Three create space for the Divine's great untangling of us. When we finally stop trying to avoid the silence, or fill it with performing or pretending, the Holy Spirit—the Spirit of truth (John 15:26)—is able to begin the work of cutting us free from the grip of our anger and fears, our competing, and our resentments. This is usually arduous and involves a lot of backtracking. The stories we love tell ourselves about our lives (catch yourself thinking off guard and you will discover what your favorite stories are) are welded into our identity, shoring us up against the world. In drawing close to the fire, all of this slowly begins to liquefy. There is an old fashioned word for this gradual change for those who follow Jesus—sanctification. This is the process of becoming more like Christ Jesus (see 2 Cor 3:4, 16–18). As this work happens within us, not by our own efforts but through the energy of the Spirit, alongside the shock of facing our toxicity, we will increasingly taste joy and peace and love because we are being liberated from what is not really us. In being re-centered in the One in whose image we are made, we will begin to know deep down homecoming and so be more able to stop playing games.

I have written elsewhere about the difficulties I experienced when I first tried to sit in quiet.[8] Let me sum up—initially I found sitting in silence impossible. I could only be (vaguely) still when I had instrumental music on in the background. It is ok to support your attempts at contemplative prayer with music or white noise if this helps to quieten your mind. It is also ok to engage with a silent practice while moving, as we will explore in chapter 5. When

---

8. See Douglas, *Jesus Sophia*, 93–94.

I first began to try and sit in silent prayer, as a university student juggling study, seeing bands, and hanging out with friends, I could only manage a few minutes of quiet at a time. However, with the repetition of returning to the silence daily, my "be still" muscles developed. Over years, and I mean *years*, I have come to relish silent retreats spread over days. It is important to note that just as you would not expect yourself to run a five kilometer marathon if you have not been running before, so you should not expect yourself to be able to engage with silence easily (even for a minute) if you have not had a practice of silent prayer before.

Start where you are. When you come to the invitations into silence in this book I encourage you to try entering into some quiet, instead of whizzing past this invitation, or thinking that you will do this another time. If silence is new for you, start with tiny chunks of quiet (there are no prizes for being a hero). Take thirty seconds or a minute to be quiet in these pauses, whether you are praying on your own or with others, or with music in the background. If it helps (and it can help) set a timer for these periods, so that you do not spend the entire time checking your watch to see if it is over. At first the quiet will probably feel like tedious nothingness. Thoughts, often annoying ones, will come up. Distractions will bombard you. Forgotten jobs will spring to mind (having paper and pen nearby to jot these down can help so that you can return to the quiet). You will probably discover that you suddenly have an itch and cannot sit still. As stated above, fresh and old wounds will start to rise to the surface of your consciousness, and this will be confronting. All of this is normal. And it is ok.

My encouragement is not to give up after a few attempts. Keep coming back to the "mat," whether you are praying in the car, a dedicated prayer space at home, in the park, or in a church. Keeping returning even when it feels like a waste of energy. Over time, if you do this, your "be still" muscles will develop as well. Many people do not feel anything when they are sitting in the silence. Instead, it continues to be a hard slog. However, over time such people might notice that they are calmer, kinder, or less reactive during the rest of the day when they maintain a practice that includes silent prayer. For others, sometimes, unexpectedly, there may be fleeting moments of beauty, or insight, or communion in the silence. Such experiences are difficult to capture in words and they cannot be made to stay. People might describe such experiences as being plunged under the surface so that they are able to see the alive mystery of grace that envelops us all of the time. Others experience a moment in which they are bathed in divine light. In such experiences people discover that where the silence felt empty, the vital, shimmering presence of the Divine is flowing. That said, the next time such a person sits in silence, prayer may well be difficult or boring all over again. Prayer practices are not circus tricks. Thankfully.

Seasons and circles

We tend to be drawn to easy solutions, competitive striving, and money-back guarantees. It therefore needs to be underscored that the spiritual life for Christians is not gym membership for the soul. Let me do this by sharing from my own journey. Between the period when I first began to sit in silence as a university student and now as I enjoy silent retreats there were also extended periods in which I could not sit at all. In one case, for a season my life was intensely full and utterly exhausting (we have twins) and I could not engage with the prayer practices that had been the bedrock of my faith. This was a complete shock. One of the challenges of this drawn-out time was to trust in God's grace, even when I could not pray as I had. For Christians, cultivating a prayer practice is not about passing a daily test, or impressing God. It is about learning how to *be* in organic, ongoing relationship with the Source of all within what is really happening for us. There will be seasons in our lives when things are going well, and seasons when events are drowning us, and still others when we feel empty (we will explore more of this in chapter 5). In the seasons that are hard we have not failed, we are standing in a different place in the circle of becoming, and the Most High, who stoops to wash our feet in Jesus, is still with us.

WORDS AND SPACES

In this chapter we have discussed the place of words and the spaces in between in prayer. Gendered language for God has been examined, the importance of reclaiming fresh and ancient imagery for the Blessed Three has been underscored, and the invitation into silence has been made. These considerations are woven into the blessings and liturgies that you will find in the pages that follow.

Part Two
Praying in Daily Life

3
Pauses in the chaos

IN THE PAGES THAT follow you will find prayers for daily life—for the morning, for midday, for evening, for when you cannot sleep, for having a cup of tea, and for other occasions. You may like to engage with one of these practices or more. These prayers seek to be organic and invitational, rather than prescriptive. It is hoped that they offer a taste of *potential* ways forward in finding a life-giving structure for prayer amidst the demands of daily life. While we are called to pray "at all times" (1 Thess 5:17) often we don't. We fall prey to the lie that our worth is based on our busyness or achievements and stay mired in worthiness competitions, and time slips away. If we wait to pray until we have got all the jobs done on the to-do list, we will often collapse at the end of day and realize that we have haven't prayed at all.

Rhythms can help to disrupt the frenetic pace that seduces and sedates us, so that we are able to become present to the Presence of love. While set liturgies can slip into speaking words by rote and tuning out, it does not have to be like this. There can be freedom within structure. Within the prayers and liturgies throughout this book, there are invitations to get real, spending time in personal prayer, and listening for the Most High. If creating a set time to pray is triggering, perhaps because of old guilt about laying aside "morning devotions," I invite you to *play*. Experiment utilizing different prayers, at different time of day. See what helps most to tune into the Holy One–Sacred Three in the fabric of your life right now.

The reason why structures are a gift in our particular context is because we live in a world that is constantly interrupting us. Notifications, emails, texts, social media feeds, and endlessly updating news cycles demand our attention and intrude upon our hearts. With the proliferation of smart phones, we are now always just a tap away from all of this. Due to the double-edged sword of the fear of missing out, and the ready dopamine hits of staying online, huge swathes of the population are forever updating their accounts. It is no accident that the language of social media coalesces with the language of drug addiction, with "feeds," "hits," and "withdrawal symptoms" all part of the common parlance. It is also no accident that there have been dramatic increases in anxiety and depression since the introduction of smart phones.[1] Having a structure that creates pauses each day—in which we put the devices down—can help to rescue us from this gargantuan force. Carving out such spaces can begin to liberate us from the lie that our value is based on our profile, and break us free from the drip-feed delusion that everyone else is having a better lunch/holiday/life than us.

To stop, whether this be in the morning with coffee, for ten minutes at lunch time, at 5:00 p.m. as we light a candle, to stop—to refuse to consume or perform—is an act of resistance. It is to reclaim our time. It is to say back to our world of demands, consumption, and attention grabbing, "I am not what I achieve." Friends, we do not need to justify our existence—it is a gift. In finding nourishing ways to pause and be open to the Divine is to rest in the shocking reality that we are a beloved of God *regardless* of our status, accomplishments, or failures. When we dare to stop, we testify to the reality that we are not the messiah. In pausing, we embody our trust in Great Spirit, who is continuing to weave the good even when we are not working.

The practical demands on our time, and the landscape of our hearts, will change dramatically in different seasons. Huge work

---

1. To explore this research, see Haidt, *Anxious Generation*.

hours, illness, caring for others, or being struck by unexpected grief, these and other things will directly impact upon what will be possible and sensible in creating a pattern for prayer and what will not. Go gently with yourself and continue to be alert to what is leading you to living waters and what is suffocating. As you look through the prayers in this chapter, it could be helpful to reflect upon what kind of season you are travelling through right now. As we are excellent at kidding ourselves that our own preferences are the Divine's preferences, it may be helpful to mull this over with a wise friend, spiritual director, mentor, minister, or small group.

PART TWO: PRAYING IN DAILY LIFE

Notes about a morning prayer

This prayer may be used regularly as a way of orienting your day. The language for the Triune God here is drawn from different strands of the biblical text and theology. The language of Author is drawn from the theological vision of the first creation account in which all things come into existence, beauty, and balance through the speaking—the telling—of the Living One. This imagery also reflects understandings in the Psalms (see Ps 139:16). The naming of the Second Person of the Trinity as the Anchor, goes back to the early church. In the letter to the Hebrews, Jesus is described as "a sure and steadfast anchor of the soul" (Heb 6:19). Crosses were not used in artwork by Christians in the beginning. This would have been a traumatizing symbol to employ when so many people, both Christians and people of other faiths, continued to be executed by the state in this agonising way. Instead, in the earliest church the symbol of the anchor was popular. The language for the Third Person of the Trinity in this prayer is drawn from John's Gospel. Here the Johannine Jesus speaks of the Spirit as the Advocate, who is "the Spirit of truth" (John 14:16-17).

There is an invitation to read a portion of a Gospel in this prayer. This Gospel reading may be from the lectionary, or you may like to read through one whole Gospel, a passage at a time, over several months. In praying the Lord's Prayer you will note the invitation to utilize a version of the prayer that speaks to your heart. See chapter 5 for further discussion of the Lord's Prayer, including samples of different versions.

The middle stanza of the morning prayer uses plural language, as the invitation is to join in prayer with, and for, Jesus followers around the globe.

A morning prayer

Beloved God, Three all Holy,
my Author, my Anchor, my Advocate,
I greet you this new morning.

> *Silence for tuning into the presence of the Divine around you and within you and for offering prayers of gratitude*

Gospel reading

> *Space after the reading for reflection*

As we embody compassion, nourish us.
As we stand against evil, empower us.
As we lift others up, uphold us.

> *Silence for prayers for others, the world, for self, and for the day's tasks*

The Lord's Prayer (in a version that speaks to your heart)

Awaken me to your presence.
Unfold your joy-full possibilities.
Make me useful in your disruptive kingdom this day.
Through Jesus, the liberator, amen.

PART TWO: PRAYING IN DAILY LIFE

Notes about a midday prayer

The central imagery of growth in this prayer is drawn from Jesus' words about the vine and branches (John 15:1–17) and from Paul's imagery of the fruit of the Spirit (Gal 5:22–25). The idea of the Divine's stubborn grace is drawn from Jesus' talk of the kingdom being like a mustard seed that grows up into a bush (Mark 4:30–32). Mustard bushes did not grow into grand trees, but rather they were tough scruffy shrubs that covered the landscape, growing in inhospitable places. What a contrast Jesus paints between the divine kingdom, like a tough shrub that creates shade for birds, and the vast empire of Rome! In the language of being re-centred, I am imagining the clay being lifted up and placed back in the middle of the wheel by the potter.

A midday prayer

Holy One–Sacred Three,
Holy Mystery, Holy Word, Holy Spirit.
Praise be to you for your presence throughout this morning.

In Jesus, you dwell with us in person,
your fullness carrying us into freedom.
Praise be to you for your unfurling restoration.

In Spirit, you cultivate love and joy and peace even amidst the stench.
So water me where I am parched, prune me as you see fit.
Praise be to you for your stubborn grace.

Holy One–Sacred Three,
in this pause I rest in you.
Re-center me in your grace.

    Silence

All glory be to you Holy One–Sacred Three.
Your love lead the way.
Through Jesus, may it be so.

PART TWO: PRAYING IN DAILY LIFE

Notes about an evening prayer

This prayer offers a pattern for marking the end of the day. It can be prayed before or after dinner, perhaps lighting a candle. The imagery of the stars having names is drawn from the Psalms (Ps 147:4). The tender imagery of the stars saying "Here we are" is from Baruch (Bar 3:34). The imagery of Jesus in this prayer is drawn from John's Gospel.

This evening prayer includes the wisdom of an awareness examen drawn from Ignatian spirituality. Taking these questions seriously and vulnerably, without trying to get the "right" answer, is an excellent resource for getting real with ourselves and with the Divine. Allow thoughts of gratitude to surface, rather than forcing ideas. Don't judge yourself for what comes up. With the second movement that focuses on times in which love was withheld, instead of seeking to solve, or blame, allow these moments to surface, without judgment, and then hand these situations over to the Source of all, seeking divine healing and grace.

This prayer includes the invitation to read one psalm a day, beginning with Psalm 1 on day one, Psalm 2 on day two, etc. This recommendation is from the theologian, author, and minister Eugene Peterson.[2] Often we only hear portions of the Psalms in church. Allowing the full intensity and rhythms of these prayers, in all their joy, sorrow, and fury to wash over us, can catapult us out of piety and help to unlock our own truths. Here, as we join in these ancient words, prayed by millions, including by Jesus (see Ps 22:1; Matt 27:46; Mark 15:34), we discover that we are not alone in our yearnings.

A fragment of Wesley's Covenant Prayer is included in the closing of this prayer.

2. In Taylor, *Open and Unafraid*, xix–xx.

An evening prayer

Composer of the universe, you name the stars;
they respond, "Here we are."

As the evening draws around
I turn to you, saying, Here I am.

For the moments of joy and love today, I give thanks.

> *Silence to contemplate these moments*

For the moments when things were ugly and love withheld, I seek your healing.

> *Silence to contemplate these moments*

Psalm

In Jesus, grace and truth are woven into skin and sinew—
vine and bread, water and shepherd.

In Spirit, you are as close as my breathing—
refreshing wind and refining fire.

Ground of our being, Water of life, Fire of truth, Blessed Three,
I am yours, and you are mine;
uphold me, infuse me, and encircle me through this night. Amen.

PART TWO: PRAYING IN DAILY LIFE

Notes on two bedtime prayers to share with children

Over the years I have struggled to find prayers to share with children that were not sickly sweet or hollow. The first short prayer is grounded in Jesus' imagery of being a mother hen (see Matt 23:37; Luke 13:34). It also draws from the Westminster Catechism with its focus on enjoying God and takes seriously that children have gifts to share in the work of the kingdom.

The second prayer to share with children draws from imagery of Jesus as the Lion and the Lamb as reflected in Revelation (Rev 5:5–6; see also John 1:29). It is also draws from language of the Nicene Creed, which describes Christ as "Light from Light."

A bedtime prayer to share with children

Jesus, we gather to you
like chicks nestling under their mother's wings.
Guard us through the night
and help us to enjoy the gift of a new day,
working with you for love.
Amen.

A prayer for a child going to sleep

Courage be yours
Peace be yours
Kindness be yours

>	all through the night
>	and into dawn

>	all through the night
>	and into dawn

In the strength of Christ Jesus—
the Lion, the Lamb, and the Light from Light.

PART TWO: PRAYING IN DAILY LIFE

Notes on the prayer before sleeping

This prayer originally appeared in *Jesus Sophia*.[3] It draws from the Wisdom Christology of Matthew's Gospel, in which Jesus is imaged as Sophia, Woman Wisdom.[4] It is grounded in Jesus Sophia's invitation to come and find rest for the soul (Matt 11:28–30; see also Sir 6:28–30; 51:23–26), and the invitation to gather under Jesus' wings (Matt 23:37). The prayer is also informed by Jesus' declaration that the birds are cared for and therefore we should stop fearing and worrying (see Matt 10:29–31; Luke 12:22–24), as well as the psalmist's celebration of the birds finding a resting place in the temple (Ps 84:1–4).

3. Douglas, *Jesus Sophia*, 156–57.
4. Douglas, *Jesus Sophia*, 34–39.

A prayer before sleeping

Three All Holy,
our source and our homecoming,
in Jesus Sophia you dwell with us,
embodying your life and way and truth:

> rest for the weary;
> nourishment for our souls;
> your love, joy, and peace.

As the globe gently spins
and birds settle in their nests
we trust in your invitation,
we gather under your wings:

> we relax;
> we put down our burdens;
> we abide in you.

Replenish our beings,
guard us through this night
and awaken us in the morning,
renewed with your wild mercy.
Amen.

PART TWO: PRAYING IN DAILY LIFE

Notes on the 3:00 a.m. despair prayer

If you spend time with the Psalms, you quickly realize how devastatingly honest the authors are with God. They tell God when they are miserable, they rage and weep. As Christians we can think, or worse, be told, that we should not be sad in dreadful times, but should just "have faith." The Psalms say otherwise. Here lament and anger are *expressions of faith*, not evidence of a lack of faith. In a world in which we are constantly told to be positive, having models for expressing our pain and sorrow are important.[5]

This prayer draws from Psalm 6. It seeks to offer one example of how we might be honest about our despair. You might like to use this psalm or find another psalm that becomes the basis of your despair prayer (see Pss 61; 77; 86; or 88). In praying these words you are not alone, but are part of a community stretching across time and space who have also keened in the night with God.

---

5. To read more about the place of lament in the church, see Douglas, Church ~~Triumphant~~ as Salt, 45–62.

3:00 a.m. despair prayer

I am weary with my moaning;
Every night I flood my bed with tears;
I drench my couch with my weeping. (Ps 6:6)

> *Space to journal, weep, listen to music, make art, . . . pour out your heart to God*

The Lord has heard my supplication;
The Lord accepts my prayer. (Ps 6:9)

PART TWO: PRAYING IN DAILY LIFE

Notes on a prayer for an enemy

In the Sermon on the Mount when Jesus calls us to pray for enemies (Matt 5:44), I do not think this is an invitation to pray for them to have a nice day. It is a call to pray for their hearts to be changed, for truth to be exposed, and for love to conquer evil. The following prayer for an enemy may be utilized for someone you know personally who has acted harmfully, misusing their power in words or deeds (or lack thereof). This prayer may also be used for political or other leaders who are misusing their power.

This prayer stands in the tradition of the Psalms (see Pss 6:10; 7:9; 9:3–10; 72:3–4). The psalmists have no qualms about expressing their anger and praying for justice to be done. This prayer includes references to the Beatitudes, in which Jesus proclaims who is actually blessed (Matt 5:1–12) and ends with the Aramaic words *marana tha* (1 Cor 16:22). When Paul uses *marana tha* or *maran atha* (there are no punctuation marks in the original Greek of the New Testament) this is suggestive of the fact that he is drawing from shared prayer practices in early Jesus communities. These words can be translated as "Our Lord, come!" (*marana tha*) or "Our Lord has come" (*maran atha*).

Prayer for an enemy

I pray for the one who does wrong . . . (*name*).
Call them to account, Most High,
smash their arrogance and ignorance upon the rocks,
break open their heart with your grace.

May those who abuse be stopped.
May those who spread hate be changed.
May the lies of the powerful be exposed,
and may justice roll down like the sea.

    Silence

Jesus, servant lord, you who herald the upsidedown kingdom,
empower the vulnerable,
energize the peacemakers,
and enliven me and all who work for justice.

Marana tha.

PART TWO: PRAYING IN DAILY LIFE

Notes on a prayer for difficult times

This is a protection prayer for when things are falling apart, or conflict is on the rise. Pausing in the midst of stressful situations and inviting divine grace into the mess is a powerful practice. In Celtic Christian tradition there are stunning prayers for protection, and the following prayer draws from this tradition. To find out more about centuries-old Celtic prayers I recommend the *Carmina Gadelica*, a collection of prayers from the Outer Hebrides of Scotland gathered by Alexander Carmichael in the 1800s.[6]

---

6. For an edited collection, see De Waal, *Celtic Vision*.

A prayer for difficult times

Blessed Three,
One Love,
amidst the strain
I long for you

    Silence

for the beauty
for the breath
for the being
I thank you

    Silence

in the pain
in the pressure
in the power-plays
I seek you

    Silence

your wisdom saturate me;
your love dispel the fear;
your presence fortify me;
through Jesus, my liberator, my healer, and my friend, I pray.

PART TWO: PRAYING IN DAILY LIFE

Notes on a tea-break prayer

This is a prayer with few words. It is about intentionally pausing to be open to the Living One. Make a favorite hot drink, leave your phone, books, pens, paper, computer aside, and go and sit somewhere kind (preferably outside). Take some moments to breathe in deeply and breathe out deeply. Pray the opening sentence and then enjoy your cup of tea, coffee, hot chocolate, etc.

    There is no technique to get wrong. Rest, breathe, notice your surroundings, the sights, smells, the feel of the seat supporting you. Let your mind wander. If people or issues come to mind, hand them to the Source of all for healing and wisdom. If things you are grateful for emerge, give thanks. *Enjoy* being with the Most High in these minutes. After five or so minutes, conclude with the words from the Psalm.

A tea-break prayer

To you I lift up my soul. (Ps 25:1)

> *Silence with a cup of something nice to help you enjoy being with the Divine*

O my God, in you I trust. (Ps 25:2)

Amen.

PART TWO: PRAYING IN DAILY LIFE

Grace before meals

For this good earth, we say:
Amen, alleluia

For wind and rain and sun, we say:
Amen, alleluia

For those who grew the food, we say:
Amen, alleluia

For those who prepared the food, we say:
Amen, alleluia

For this time together, we say:
Amen, alleluia

For your presence, Christ, among us we say:
Amen, alleluia

Strengthen us and all who work for justice, we say:
Amen, alleluia

So your feast may be shared with all! And we say:
Amen, alleluia
Amen.

4
Blessings in living and dying

THE LANGUAGE OF BLESSING is both under- and overused in our global village. In social media posts, people talk about being *#blessed*, as they overtly boast or humble-brag about their radiant skin, house, or children. This idea of blessing has little to do with the way of Jesus, and has lot more to do with consumerism and the pursuit of status. In contrast to the endlessly futile attempts people make to emulate the constructed lives of influencers, Jesus says being blessed looks very different. In the Sermon on the Mount, Jesus offers a summary of who is blessed (Matt 5:1–12). Contrary to expectations, Jesus says that the blessed are those who are poor in spirit. Jesus says the blessed are those who mourn, because they will be comforted. Jesus says the blessed are vulnerable and transparent and kind. Jesus says those who are hungry for justice to be established are blessed, because they will be filled. Jesus says blessed are those who do the hard work of engaging in conflicted spaces and building peace. According to Jesus, people are blessed when they are persecuted for working for justice, or when they are hassled or maligned for being part of the Jesus movement. These ideas of blessing are very different from contemporary constructs of a blessed life.

I once received a very strange and beautiful blessing. This was not like the saccharine *#blessed* posts of social media. It was more like the disruptive blessings Jesus speaks about. I was in my twenties and had recently walked away from a toxic context. I was left ragged and rattled. I wanted to stay home. Cocooned. I did not have the energy to talk to people, especially to strangers. Despite this, one day soon after, I had to run an errand. No car was available, and so I travelled by public transport. On the tram I kept myself to myself. This was until an old, dishevelled woman started speaking. People instantly became fascinated by something in the middle distance, averting their gaze. Somehow the old lady caught my eye, she fished around in her bag, and pulled something out, saying "There is evil in the world, you need to protect yourself." She then thrust a Catholic medallion towards me and said: "This is for protection." I could feel people surreptitiously watching to see how I would react, curious and relieved that they had not been the targeted recipient of this gift. I accepted the medallion with thanks.

Young, Protestant, and, at that time having very little exposure to Roman Catholic traditions, I would normally have been deeply suspicious of such an object. However in that moment, amidst the ricocheting impacts of trauma, this old woman spoke directly into the truth of my experience—she bore witness—and the medallion was a gift. Now this is the thing, this blessing from a stranger did not take away the suffering. I still had to attend to the pain and this took time and work, and the support of others. And yet, the words and actions of this eccentric stranger made a difference to me. She was an angel in disguise when I was in the wilderness. She named the truth, and she called upon the Divine's protecting and healing presence for me right in that moment. There was power in this blessing. I still have the medallion.

What might it mean to reclaim the place of blessing *within* the mess of life? Despite the endless boasty posts, a blessed life will not always be #awesome. It is a lie that if we bless someone, suffering will be eradicated. The opposite conclusion, that blessing achieves nothing, is also a lie. Jesus says *blessing exists in the midst of the pain* when things are not perfect—within our grieving, our attempts at being merciful, our aching for justice, our struggles to build peace, and when we are hated. Imagine if we took this seriously. What would blessings be like? The Irish writer John

O'Donohue speaks about the power of blessing, stating: "A blessing is a circle of light drawn around a person to protect, heal, and strengthen."[1] I cherish this imagery. This is what the old woman on the tram did for me. The suffering was still there, but in her words and actions she bore witness to this reality *and* encircled me with divine light.

To understand blessing in this way is to step away from the lie that terrible things don't happen to #*blessed* people. To understand blessing in this way disrupts the infantile and deeply damaging idea that if we have enough faith or are a good enough person, everything will be miraculously sorted out. This is Santa propaganda, not the way of Jesus. The One at the heart of our faith does not have an easy or awesome life. In the Gospels we are told that Jesus, the God One, is derided, deserted, and allows himself to be falsely detained and executed by the empire. We follow the Holy Human One, the beloved, who does not make things easy with the flick of a fairy wand but who, instead, enters into our experiences of trauma, betrayal, misunderstanding, and grief. What is more, Jesus is utterly honest about the reality that if we choose to walk with him, it will not bring ease, wealth, or popularity. Instead, it will be difficult and costly (see Matt 5:10–12; Mark 8:34–35; 10:41–45). Christian understandings of blessing are very different from the world's.

To bless someone from the kind of terrain Jesus speaks from is to recognize the truth—that terrible things are happening *and* that the Divine is actively present, working for liberation, healing, and new life in the midst of the pain. We are people of the cross and resurrection. We are called to hold together the truth of the devastation of Good Friday, the emptiness of Holy Saturday, and the unexpectedness of Easter Day. To bless from this space is to honor the tears and rage and despair *and* to draw divine light—that cannot be overcome by the darkness—around a person, or situation, at the same time (see John 1:5).

This understanding is reflected in the blessing from Ephesians cited in chapter 2. As people in Jesus communities seek to

---

1. O'Donohue, *To Bless This Space Between Us*, 198.

be faithful in the midst of increasing hostility from the wider community and the state, magical solutions are not prayed for. Instead, the writer states:

> I pray that, according to the riches of his glory, he may grant that you may be strengthened in your *inner being* with power through his Spirit. (Eph 3:16)

May your inner being be strengthened. This is a blessing I would gladly receive any day.

To offer an authentic Christian blessing is to recognize the awfulness of what someone is going through, without trying to cheer them up, or fix things (see Rom 12:15). It is a call to bear witness to the pain, while drawing our strength from the Divine who enters into our suffering in Christ Jesus. To bless someone in such a way is to trust that the Triune God is present and can pour strength and wisdom, grace and creativity, peace and even hope—but not manufactured movie endings—into the situation, and to share this. However, it is a gift that calls for humility and the open acknowledgement that the person we seek to bless may choose to close themselves off from the blessing (at least for now), and that this is ok. We will discuss this, and the contours of intercessory prayer, in chapter 8.

A blessing can be offered to someone within a conversation or pastoral-care encounter, for example, when a person has received terrible news about their health, or a loved one. Blessings can also be shared as part of worship (with peoples' permission beforehand) at a time of transition, for example in new beginnings. Blessings can also be shared via email and post. Delivered in this way, people can choose to read a blessing in their own time, and engage with, or reject, the blessing in their own way. In seasons of uncertainty, ill-health, and great suffering, often peoples' autonomy is severely limited. Actively respecting peoples' choice at such a time can be a gift in itself. We do not need to know the outcomes. We can simply (and profoundly) offer a blessing as a witness to love amidst the suffering without expectations. This is what the woman on the tram did for me.

Notes on the blessings

In this chapter you will find blessings for various occasions. These blessings are grounded in the shocking conviction that in Christ Jesus, God enters the mess of our living and dying, embodying gracious, non-retaliatory power and light that cannot be overcome by violence or death.

In some of these blessings you will find references to the fragrance of Christ. While perhaps unfamiliar, this evocative imagery is found in Paul's second letter to the community in Corinth (2 Cor 2:15–17).

The blessing for one hurt by the church draws from Matthew 10:26 (see also Mark 4:22; Luke 12:2), and from the Nicene Creed.

PART TWO: PRAYING IN DAILY LIFE

A blessing for parents whose baby is unwell in the womb

As you reel from the shock of doctors' words
that fling you to the edge of the abyss where death demands attention—
may there be one or two brave souls
who will stand with you there in that lonely place.

In the endless waiting
for test results, between scans, for days to crawl by—
in the spaces in between breathing in and breathing out,
may you cherish the quiet wonder and beauty of your child.

As you contend with the endless images of happy families,
may you know the dignity and preciousness of your baby—
this little one in your family
who is fearfully and wonderfully made.

As you weep, may you know God weeping with you,
holding you in her tender arms—
catching the tears,
honoring your grief.

And may you know, deep in your being, however this path unfolds,
that your baby is held in love
in this life and the life to come.

A blessing for a new role

As you stand on the shore of this adventure,
grieving what you leave behind, energized by what is ahead,
may you know a quiet strength.

As the old falls away, with its clarity and rhythms,
and you are left in the vulnerability of the unknown,
may you have the courage to be yourself and to wait.

May you draw from the deep well of your experience,
knowing that nothing is lost
and may saints—living and dead—accompany you along the way.

And as you slowly find your footing,
may you continue to seek grace and truth
so that you are able to notice and share the fragrance of Christ in this new place.

PART TWO: PRAYING IN DAILY LIFE

A blessing for someone who is lonely

When the world closes in and you feel alone,
when it seems that those around you speak a different language
and there is no room for you,
may you find somewhere safe to grieve.

When cynicism has become your bedfellow,
when your defences repel others
and the stories you tell are centred on rejection,
may you be interrupted by grace.

May the vast night skies ground you in wonder.
May the music of birds remind you of a deeper song.
May you notice the smile of a stranger
and be open to the possibility that it is real.

May you let the Spirit near your wounds.
May you experiment with being kind to yourself and to others.
And when a soul-friend crosses your path,
may you dare to take a step forward.

A blessing for a teenager

In this time of upheaval and growth,
as your beauty and being are awkwardly unfolding
and there is much beyond your control,
may you delight in the sacred ordinary:
—the joy of being silly;
—the energy of caring for others and the earth;
—good books, loud music, and delicious food.

As the world tells you what you should be,
and you are bombarded with filtered faces,
may you have the courage to turn away,
knowing that your worth does not come from others.
May you find your own voice
and stand in your own strength
as a beloved child of God.

As simplistic ideas about religion begin to fall away
and questions rise to the surface,
may you know that this is not the sound of your faith dying
but the call to dive more deeply.
May young and old friends attend to you with respect.
May you discover fresh springs as you wrestle with the way of Jesus.
And may you glimpse that the Most High has dreams for you in this beautiful, broken world.

PART TWO: PRAYING IN DAILY LIFE

A blessing for one whose child has died as a result of violence

When violence steals your child
the ground beneath you falls away,
the things you trusted lie in rubble.
A gaping space screams between your outstretched arms
where your darling one should be.
The presence of the absence of God leaves you numb.

In the agony of this grief
may you weep the tears that threaten to suffocate you.
May you find ways to express the fury well.
May you be strengthened in your work for justice.
Somehow, sometimes, may there be moments of peace—
as you return to the deep knowing that your beloved is now safe.

As day falls into day,
while you continue to carry this excruciating burden,
may unexpected angels tend to you
in the guise of strangers, neighbors, dogs, and birds.
Somehow, sometimes, may there be moments of grace—
when beauty surprises you with its whisper that there may yet be new life.

And in the gap between the words,
when there is nothing left to say,
may the fragrance of the Holy Human One—
who enters our hells and whose love is stronger than death—
somehow, sometimes, reach you,
bearing the hope-suffused scent that today is not the end of the story.

A blessing for when the church fails you

When your dreams are dashed
and the songs about loving one another
taste like acid on your tongue,
may Jesus, the Anointed One, stand by you.

When your assumptions about people acting in kindness
are shredded by the self-absorption of Christians,
when there are no consequences for those who do wrong,
may you be strengthened in your inner being.

When you fear that there is no real church left,
when you need allies to discern how and when to call for justice,
may you find true friends, perhaps in those around you, perhaps
in the pages of old.
May Spirit empower you in the waiting and in the advocating, and
knowing what time this is.

In the fury, sorrow, and frustration,
may you draw comfort in the reality that truth will out.
What is done in darkness will be exposed
and the Lamb who is our liberator and judge will have the final
word.

PART TWO: PRAYING IN DAILY LIFE

A blessing for entering a shopping center

As I enter this temple, guard me.
Protect me from unnecessary buying.
Shield me from incessant advertising.
Defend me from the fear that I am not—and do not have—enough.

May I notice and smile at the lonely.
May I speak kindly to the shop assistant.
May I thank the cleaners.
And may I buy products that are made fairly.

And in my presence in this building,
may I testify to the alternate reign of your love,
in which the last will be first
and the kingdom belongs to the poor.

A blessing for a person being ordained

As you are called to stand in a new place
may you savor the seriousness of the ordination charge:
You are called to be a story-keeper of the good tidings of Jesus.

Remember that you are set apart—not above others—to have extended time
to be undone and remade by sacred text and the Divine, week by week:
Pay attention to the gospel, the world, the overlooked, and to what the Spirit is whispering.

You are promising to live close to the fire
you will be burned as you grow, the old must give way for new life
Help others to recognize, and dwell close to, the life-giving flames.

Do not fall for the lie that you must have all the answers
make room for the questions within you and others:
Create space to explore together.

Thankfully you are not the messiah!
You are part of the communion of saints, living and dead:
Participate in the Spirit's birthing that is already growing around you and within.

And may prayer, like a creek, quietly flow through your days
sustaining you in seasons of despair and joy:
So that people may glimpse the love that is stronger than death wherever you go.

PART TWO: PRAYING IN DAILY LIFE

A blessing upon receiving a terminal diagnosis

As time is burst apart,
when life is irrevocably divided between before and after,
may you ponder what you need, desire, and long to share—and pursue this.

When regrets threaten to drown you,
may you find paths towards forgiving yourself
and freeing others.

When you are terrified for those you leave behind,
may you find ways to share honestly with one another
and allow supports to gather close.

As people avoid you, afraid that they may catch death like a cold,
may true friends, new and old, step forward to walk you home.
And may there be moments of delight and rest.

May your longings and lament find a listening place in the Source of all.
May the One who goes to hell and back for us uphold you—
offering the light and showing the way.

A blessing for waiting

In this in-between time,
as you long for clarity,
unable to move forward on the path,
may you know in your being that waiting is a form of action too.

May there be peace in the unknown,
wisdom in the discerning,
creativity in the listening,
and patience in this pause.

May wise companions hold space with you,
brave companions ask questions with you,
hopeful companions gently laugh with you,
and may steadfast companions pray with you.

And in the time,
when the "Yes" of the Divine and "yes" of your heart meet,
may clarity take shape with a steady sureness
so that you may get up and walk ahead,
with humility, strength, and joy.

5

When there are no words

SOMETIMES WE CANNOT PRAY. Or, more accurately, we cannot pray as we used to. The words have dried up. You may be in such a season right now. I have been there. Our babies were born very prematurely. A dear friend says the "parents of preemies club" is not a club you would wish your worst enemies to be in. She is right. It is almost impossible to convey what this experience is like to those who have not been through it. Conversely, strangers and I have bonded instantly after discovering that we have both had babies in a Neonatal Intensive-Care Unit over an extended period of time. For months my partner and I lived with myriad unpredictable challenges, from emergency life-threatening operations, being unable to hold our babies, the din of oxygen-saturation alarms, endless assessments, infections, insensitive commentaries, and midnight phone calls to the ward. We travelled through this season with no guarantees and with little power or agency along the way.

A few days after our babies were born, while I was still a hospital patient myself, I walked into the NICU ward where one precious intensive-care nurse was assigned to look after each tiny patient, and I began to inwardly pray. In that moment I *felt* a voice. I did not hear the voice of God like in the movies. This was non-auditory. Instead, these words were expressed within me: "You do not need to pray, other people are praying—just be with your babies." So I did. Each day my partner and I would spend hours by their plastic humidity cribs, with nurses always present, monitors always pulsating, and specialists coming and going without warning. We would talk with our babies, sing to them, and read to them. When we were allowed to touch them, we would hold their hands, and finally, as they grew stronger, we could hold them close in kangaroo cuddles. In all of this I did not attempt to pray. I put this aside and let other people do this. I could feel the prayers surrounding us. In this season I crashed into the reality that there are times when we do not have the words, or the energy, to pray.

Thankfully, our babies were released from hospital, eventually. However, my prayer life did not bounce back. This was extremely difficult for me. The hard-won contemplative practices, which I had established over years, were gone. I could not sit in silence in the morning or in the evening as I had done. I was exhausted all of the time as we continued to care for our babies day and night, mostly living in isolation on the advice of specialists. I wondered, when I had a second, who I was if I did not pray. I wrestled with whether prayer could look different in this season. Could prayer be expressed in the form of being present to the wonder of these little ones? Could prayer be embodied in focused attention—loving them, delighting in them, and caring for them in each moment, as Mother Father God does for us?

Looking back I see that this was a form of prayer. Being attentive, in gratitude and love, within the relentless minutiae of feeding, soothing, nappy changing, being tenderly present amidst the health scares and fitful sleep—all of this was praying. During this season I was flung entirely upon the grace of the Divine, moment by moment. While this may sound like a beautiful expression of prayer, this was hard to accept at the time. I missed the rhythms of my old prayer life. I yearned for the silence and for time for deep reflection. I continued to struggle with questions about my identity as a disciple of Jesus in this new space.

Alongside the discombobulation brought about by the obliteration of my old prayer practices, something else emerged that was equally confronting. I came to recognize that I had drawn a sense of pride from my contemplative rhythms. I began to recognize that in some ways the practices of contemplation had become an idol. I began to see that we humans, me included, have an inordinate capacity to avoid contact with the Living God. While we do this in obvious ways, such as through busyness, scrolling, or accumulation, I was confronted with the reality that even a prayer practice can become a distraction from being *with* God, and instead can become a righteous habit, and foul fodder for the ego. This was humbling, to say the least.

For a significant period I could not pray as I had. However, while I longed for the "mat," the sky didn't fall just because I was not sitting in silence. The One who calls each of us by name was faithful. I did not need to earn my place in this relationship. When this season eventually shifted, and I was slowly able to reclaim beloved prayer practices, I was changed by my *extended* time in the desert—for the better. I was less rigid, more compassionate (towards myself and towards others), and more alive to the reality that it really is *not* up to us. Grace is moving like a river, forever and always, and we can be open to this in so many ways. Or not. The grace still flows.

The reality that sometimes times we cannot pray—or pray in ways that we once loved—is not spoken about in the church very often. However, for many reasons this is a common experience for people. Sometimes there is no time or capacity to pray because of the demands on our attention to care for others, or because of our own serious illness. At times, our spiritual life becomes dried out, crushed by the weight of grief, disappointment, depression, anxiety, or rage. While our babies came home, other people endure the horror of the death of their babies, or other beloved people. We need to get better at talking about these realities in faith communities, without shaming or deriding one another or ourselves. We need to stop assuming that if we, or someone else, cannot pray in a way we recognize, that this indicates failure at being a Christian, or a lack of faith. We need to normalize the reality that the spiritual journey is like a circle rather than an escalator. It will include times of desolation and despair, as well as times of consolation and joy. The Psalms graphically express this truth. This chapter is about the times when we have no words.

There are as many ways to pray as there are to listen and communicate in our daily interactions. As shown in various studies, our non-verbal cues often convey the greatest meaning. A tone, a look, a slump of the shoulders, the crossing of our arms, turning away while someone is talking, all of these non-verbal ways of speaking communicate volumes. Moving beyond the idea that prayer—our communication with God—must always involve articulating words is both truthful and emancipatory. We don't have to explain everything. Our inner beings long for refreshment, just as a deer longs for the stream (Ps 42:1–3), and at times this thirst is beyond the confines of language. When Paul, the bombastic early church leader, writes to the Jesus community in Rome, he makes this point with exquisite gentleness:

> Likewise the Spirit helps us in our weakness; for we do not know how to pray as we ought, but that very Spirit intercedes with sighs too deep for words. (Rom 8:26)

Can we imagine putting down our carefully crafted words, our striving, and our guilt about not being able to pray, and allow the Spirit to sigh within us, giving expression to our deepest longings?

In the pages that follow we will explore diverse prayer practices that move beyond more familiar styles of prayer, which rely on speaking. You may resonate with some of these ideas. They may connect for a season, or they might prompt you to search out, or create, other prayer styles. If you look in bookshops, you will be able to find works by various authors about each of the following suggested ways of praying. However, before you turn the page, it needs to be underscored that there may be times, like the one I lived through, in which nothing, no practice, is going to help. If the suggestions in this chapter do not resonate, this does not mean that all is lost. Faith is not about earning merit badges. There are no "three easy steps" to spiritual ease. You are beloved whether you feel it or not.

PART TWO: PRAYING IN DAILY LIFE

Prayer walking

Research findings in health continue to demonstrate that there are many rich benefits for our minds and bodies in going for a walk. Endorphins are released, blood is pumped more quickly through our veins, we benefit from being outside, and we become fitter. Walking is also free and no special equipment is required. It is less risky than high-impact sports, and if we are able to use our legs, walking is immediately available, even if our fitness levels are low. Walking draws us out of our own heads and into the fullness of who we are as *embodied* beings. Walking also draws us into a wider perspective, as we become present to our surrounds, whether this be our neighborhood, or the park, or a path along the creek. Prayer walking invites us to become attentive to the world around us and to the Composer of all.

Pilgrimage—walking as prayer—has been part of Christian practice for countless centuries. Within Jewish tradition, the bedrock of Christian faith, making pilgrimage to the temple in Jerusalem was an essential practice of faith and prayer. Not only is this reflected in the Psalms (see, for example, the songs of ascent in Psalms 120–34), we also see it in the Lukan account of Mary and Joseph, as we glimpse their faith practices (see Luke 2:22–51). While some opine about the decline of formal religion, it is curious that the popularity of making pilgrimage has found a resurgence in recent decades. Both people of faith and people who claim no faith are increasingly engaging in intentional, sacred walks. While cost, or distance, may hinder many of us from making pilgrimage to the Holy Land, or along the Santiago De Compostela pilgrimage in Spain, we can still engage with walking as a spiritual practice, even in our own (scruffy or leafy) neighborhoods.

Prayer walks can be practiced in different ways. Here I will outline two approaches. We can engage with prayer walking as a practice of attention, in which we seek to be open to our surrounds, to ourselves, and to the presence of the Most High as we walk. We can begin our walk with a word or gesture that symbolizes our openness to the movement of the Holy Spirit. Then as we walk, we tune in. We tune in to the beauty, we allow our thoughts to wander, we are open to the insights that emerge as we listen and look. Creative solutions may begin to hatch, people may come to mind whom we feel prompted to pray for or follow up, gratitude may flow. This prayer practice is organic, embodying a posture of lively trust in the Living One who is present and moving as we move.

A different way to engage with prayer walking is to use this practice as a way of intentionally praying for others. As you walk, you pray for your neighbors. You might do this on the local level. For example, when you pass the school, the shop, the retirement village, or the house with the broken window, you pray for those whose lives are part of these places. Alternatively, you can utilize prayer walking to pray for different parts of the world. As you reach different landmarks, perhaps when you pass the house with the blue door, you pray for a particular war zone and for peace to be established, or when you pass that big old tree you pray for greater care for the environment. Such praying does not require words. At each landmark you might imagine love and light flowing through you to each of these situations (see chapter 8 for detailed discussion of intercessory prayer).

Prayer walking is often best done in silence, so that we can truly tune in. However, there may be times when you might need music as part of your prayer walk (read on to explore this). Finding, or creating, your own pilgrimage site for your walk can also be an anchor. This may not be a particularly noticeable place to others. It might be a rusty seat in a park, or a rock beside the river, or a particular tree. Making pilgrimage part of you own prayer life connects you with the communion of saints and can be a powerful, grounding, ongoing gift.

Walking the labyrinth is another way of engaging with prayer walking (if you are unable to walk, engaging with a finger labyrinth on paper or wood can be powerful). It is not entirely clear where, or why, labyrinths were first used. However, in contemporary context their popularity continues to grow. There is a stunning labyrinth in Chartres Cathedral, and its pattern has been copied the world over.

There may be a labyrinth near you in a church, a retreat center, or outdoors. A labyrinth is not a maze. There is only one way in and one way out. There are no tricks and you will not get lost if you just keep putting one foot in front of the other. Walking the labyrinth as an expression of prayer can enable deep communion with the Source of all. It can be powerful to begin by naming your desire to God, or by choosing some words from the biblical text to take with you in the walking. As the path unfolds, and you journey to the center, and then return, the invitation is to walk mindfully and to listen. Sometimes we are able to hear things that have been buried deep down within us. There are labyrinth networks the world over that you may wish to connect with. Walking the labyrinth can be an astonishing way to engage with prayer walking.

Sitting still

In complete contrast to wordy prayers, and the practice of prayer walking, cultivating the capacity to sit still and listen is a powerful way to pray. Within these lands called Australia, First Nation leaders offer deep wisdom about this kind of watching and attending. Indigenous leader, artist, storyteller, and educator Miriam-Rose Ungunmerr-Baumann shares about the practice of Dadirri, a word from the Ngan'gikurunggurr and Ngen'giwumirri nations. Ungunmerr Baumann states: "Dadirri recognises the deep spring that is inside us. We call on it and it calls to us."[1] In learning from the wisdom of First Nation elders, frenetic and frazzled non-indigenous peoples may yet be saved from their busyness.

In learning to sit still, either outside or at a special prayer place that we create in our home, perhaps, with an icon and candle, we stop trying to fill the silences, impress the Divine, or solve our own, or everyone else's, problems. Here we can put down our superhero capes, and all our other deluded ego trips, and listen. Learning how to actually be present, in our good bodies, in the moment, on ancient soil is a profound challenge. It is also a profound gift. Can

---

1. Miriam-Rose Foundation, "Dadirri."

you imagine learning to be open to what the Divine may speak to you, through art, your senses, or imagination, through a bird, or animal, or tree? This is hard, transformative work. To begin to be open, we must push through the desire to control, or to be entertained, two very seductive idols in our culture.

Whether you are experiencing a time of consolation or desolation, this prayer style can be a gift. You may like to decide on a particular place to begin experimenting with this practice. Try not to be judging yourself and point scoring the entire time. Begin to notice your body, where you hold tension, and relax that space. As suggested in chapter 3's "Tea break prayer," you may want to begin this time of deeper listening by greeting the Most High. Alternatively, you may opt to use no words but gestures instead, such as bowing your head, or crossing yourself, as you begin. Remember this is not a competition, and the outcomes may not be perceivable for some time. But if we open the door of our heart, the Holy One, who is there waiting, will enter with healing—and probably with some table-turning as well.

Prayer journaling

While praying with set liturgies can bring life, and developing prayer practices that focus on silence can be transformative, these prayer styles might feel suffocating for some people or for some of the time. For those who are more comfortable writing about their thoughts than speaking them, journaling can be a life-giving form of prayer. In prayer journaling, the invitation is to write bluntly about what is going on for you and to invite the Divine into this jumble. This kind of journaling is not for public consumption. Nor are such patterns of journaling-as-prayer about documenting the day's activities, or recording achievements. Here permission is given to include confused and brittle thoughts and unvarnished emotions, including all the stupid things driving you to distraction, both within yourself and in others. Raw prayers such as "help me now" or "clarity please" might be scribbled down. You might write about your hopes, joys, fears, fury, or that persistent clash with a loved one. Such journals are often messy, and it can be better to write in a regular lecture notebook rather than a beautifully bound volume. This takes the pressure off.

This kind of journaling might include reflections on dreams, the gathering up of those things you are grateful for each day, quotes from a Bible passage or a work of theology, all alongside your own reflections and the longings of your heart. If you keep such a journal over an extended period of time, there is wisdom in reading back. You may discover key insights that have been growing over some time, or recurring themes that demand attention. You may like to highlight these and discuss them with a trusted friend, spiritual director, or mentor. Often we are strangers to ourselves unless we do the deep hard work with the Author of life. Journaling regularly can help us to do this work, leading to greater wisdom about what is going on within us, and what the Divine is longing for us.

Art making

We are so much more than the words we use. By engaging with art as a form of prayer, our inner being is able to commune with the Great Artist. You don't have to be artistic to make art part of your prayer practice. While you may be shy to take up watercolors, oil, or acrylics, what might it be like to try? This art-making is not for others to see. You need no one else's approval. You don't need to go to classes to engage with art as prayer. Three-year-old children are confident that they can draw and paint, and they are right. Engaging with this prayer style is perhaps in part an invitation to re-connect with our inner child. Beyond the inner and outer critics that stymie us, in making art we may be more able to respond to Jesus' insistent call to become like an infant and *receive* the kingdom like a child (see Matt 18:4; Mark 10:15; Luke 18:17; John 3:3). When we are no longer trying to impress with being the "best," there is more chance that we will actually be honest *and* receptive.

Making art as an expression of prayer—whether making sketches in a scrapbook, taking photographs in nature, arranging flowers, or sculpting—is about abiding in, and enjoying, the presence of the Creator of all. Collage can be an excellent "safe" way of making art. Here the focus is on using pictures or words from magazines or other sources to make a piece that expresses your prayer—your desire, your hope, or your longing. Working with mandalas—whether coloring in patterns or making a mandala on the beach out of shells and seaweed—can be a form of meditative prayer. Exploring a theme, a question, or a passage from the Bible with art can be a way of engaging all of our senses more deeply as we tune in to the Divine. In our world, which is obsessed with outcomes, it may feel frivolous to make art that will not be seen by others. This prayer style, however, is between you and God. This practice challenges us to lay down the demands of our performative culture and instead be vulnerable to what is real and lasting.

Imaginative contemplation

In *Jesus Sophia* I write about contemplative prayer practices, including lectio divina and imaginative prayer.[2] Both of these prayer styles, in different ways, invite people to pray with passages from the biblical text. When prayer feels dead, these practices may offer a path towards living waters. For those of us who are Protestant, this may be particularly so, because alongside the gifts of the Reformation, we have unfortunately tended to reduce our engagement with the biblical text to a form of analysis in which we seek the (one) right answer. This can lead to both our inner life and the Bible feeling flat. However, it must be underscored, as stated in *Jesus Sophia*, these practices do not replace the importance of rigorous biblical analysis. As a New Testament scholar, I am passionate about this crucial, ongoing, intellectual work. There is room for academic analysis and for contemplative prayer.

Here, I will give a taste of imaginative contemplation (or imaginative composition), a practice informed by Ignatian spirituality. This practice begins with becoming still before the Most

---

2. Douglas, *Jesus Sophia*, 94–96. See also Hansen, *Gospels for Prayer*, or explore Ignatian spirituality websites.

High, aware of what we desire, and naming this to God. Then a small portion of a Gospel is read and engaged with *imaginatively*, as the name suggests. This is different to secular patterns of guided meditation, in which leading questions encourage people to visualize specific things in order to reach a certain state of mind or being. Instead, in imaginative contemplation the questions are open-ended, inviting people to engage and respond freely to the Gospel reading.

In imaginative contemplation, the questions are informed by the passage and invite us to engage with the senses. For example, we might read Mark 6:30–44 and then ask ourselves:

- How do the disciples look as they report back to Jesus?
- Jesus invites them to come away. What is the boat like?
- What do you see and smell as you sail?
- On shore, what does this deserted place look like?
- Who is in this great crowd?
- What do you hear?
- How does Jesus respond to the crowd?
- What are you doing?
- It is late and the disciples tell Jesus to send the crowds away. How do they seem?
- Jesus says, "You give them something to eat." How do they react to these words? How do you react these words?
- Who finds the loaves?
- Jesus takes the five loaves and two fish, looks up to heaven, then blesses them and breaks them. What is this like?
- Jesus gives the loaves and fishes to the disciples to give out. How do the people receive these gifts?
- What are you doing?
- All ate and were filled. What is the atmosphere like?

After responding to the questions, the invitation is to ponder what has emerged for you, and to converse with the Holy One–Sacred Three about this experience.

The basic structure above can be utilized with any small portion of a Gospel reading, tailoring the questions to the particular scene, but always with open-ended questions that draw us to our sensory responses. Like all prayer styles in Christian tradition, this is not a test or about getting it "right." At times, remarkable insights about yourself, about the Scriptures, and about Jesus' call to you, cut through the waffling and worrying. At other times, engaging with this prayer style will feel empty. There is always tomorrow or the next day. The Spirit is moving, and the Divine's grace remains steady even while we fluctuate.

Singing and dancing (while no one is watching)

Music has been integral to religion through the centuries and across cultures. In Judeo-Christian tradition the Psalms form a core song book for us to utilize. Rather beautifully, the author of Colossians encourages early Jesus communities to "sing psalms, hymns, and spiritual songs to God" (Col 3:16), not just as a nice idea, but as a core expression of faithfulness. I love this invitation. Rather than music being a secondary component of life, imagine if we took seriously that singing and music were integral aspects of our ongoing relationship with God? When we are in seasons in which we cannot pray with words, or in quietness, music can be an amazing medium for being with the Divine.

In inviting us to think about music as prayer, I am not only talking about uplifting worship music or traditional hymns. While these styles of music may be life-giving for some, for others such music is stultifying. Furthermore, while in Colossians the encouragement is to express gratitude in song, the Psalms also remind us that there is a need to express our rage and sorrow in song. In times of despair, loud techno or rock, reggae or soulful folk or jazz may be the mediums that express our longings—our prayers—most faithfully. Whatever style of music speaks to you right now, can you imagine letting music be a way of praying? Can you imagine choosing music that expresses your longings to God, making a play list, and letting this be your prayer? Could you imagine dancing or singing, or stomping along the pavement, or driving with this music blaring *as* your way of being with God and being yourself? If this is a new thought for you, it could be time to try.

The prayer of resistance

I would like to conclude this exploration with the prayer of resistance that Jesus taught. In a chapter focused on how we might pray when there are no words, it may seem odd to end with a specific set of words. However, when we are struggling to find our own words for prayer, the Lord's Prayer can be a gift. This prayer goes back to accounts of how Jesus taught people to pray (see Matt 6:8-15; Luke 11:1-4). This prayer has been, and is, prayed by countless millions of people around the globe. For early Reformers—including Martin Luther, John Calvin, and John Knox—praying the Lord's Prayer is essential to the practice of faith because, as Calvin states, Christ "supplies words for our lips."[3] Sometimes we do not have to be original, we can simply join in the splendid chorus.

There is multilayered power in the Lord's Prayer. Here Jesus calls us to resist the empires of the world, as we pray for the inbreaking of God's disruptive reign. To pray this prayer is to assert that there is One God, who has the ultimate power—the true kingdom—therefore, all other human powers and systems are relativized. What is more, if the Divine is our true father (and mother) who longs to feed us and free us, we are liberated from all patriarchal (and kyriachal) constructions of power.[4] No other

---

3. Calvin, *Institutes*, III.20.34.

4. Elisabeth Schüssler Fiorenza coined the term "kyriarchy," drawing from the Greek words for "lord" or "master" (*kyrios*) and "to rule or dominate" (*archein*). With this term, Schüssler Fiorenza underscores that there are a "complex social pyramid of graduated dominations and subordinations" in societies, and that these pyramidic structures are not simply bound by gender. Schüssler Fiorenza, *Jesus*, 14.

person, whether in our family, church, or government, can have true authority over us.

It can be difficult the catch the scent of dissent in this prayer because of the polite and often mindless recitation of these words in churches, and other institutions. This was not the case in the beginning. In the midst of living under the cruel occupation of Rome, Jesus was teaching followers to pray for another kingdom to come. This is tantamount to treason. Within the Didache, an early church text likely written sometime in the late first century, Jesus communities are encouraged to pray this prayer three times a day (Did. 8). This would have been a brave thing to do with Roman soldiers stationed nearby. It still is. To pray this prayer is to declare that our allegiance is not to the empire or to any particular political party. To pray this prayer is to claim trust in a higher force, and to testify to the reality that despite the hurts and systemic injustices, God is present and coming. It is to testify to the reality that the Most High longs to nourish each of us with the bread we need, and to lead us into the kind of experiential freedom in which fear, scarcity, and bitterness are dispelled.

While this prayer of resistance is magnificent, there are, however, significant blocks that preclude people engaging with these words in our contemporary context. Not only has the meaning of the prayer been drained because of over-familiarity, the language of the prayer is also a barrier to many. The words are too male, and they sound too much like an endorsement, rather than a disruption, of empire-shaped power. If this is the case for you, there are alternate versions of the Lord's Prayer to explore. Jim Cotter, an Anglican priest, has written versions of the Lord's Prayer. Here is one:

> Life-Giver, Pain-Bearer, Love-Maker,
>   Source of all that is and that shall be,
> Father and Mother of us all,
>   Loving God, in whom is heaven:
>
> The hallowing of your name echo
>   through the universe!
> The way of your justice be followed
>   by all peoples of the world!

PART TWO: PRAYING IN DAILY LIFE

> Your heavenly will be done
>   by all created beings!
> Your commonwealth of peace and freedom
>   sustain our hope and come on earth.
>
> With the bread that we need for today, feed us.
> In the hurts we absorb from one another forgive us.
> In times of temptation and test, strengthen us.
> From trials too great to endure, spare us.
> From the grip of all that is evil, free us.
>
> For you reign in the glory of the power that is love,
> now and forever, amen.[5]

Within the Australian context, Denise Champion—Indigenous leader, theologian, and Uniting Church minister—has written an Adnyamathanha translation of the Lord's Prayer:

> Our Father
> Who lives in heaven
> Your name is big
> Your name is good
> Your Holy land is coming
> That's the way God does things
> On earth and in heaven.
> Give us today our special bread
> Make things right for humankind when we do the wrong thing by God.
>
> We make things right for others who do the wrong thing against us.
> Do not take us on the bad road
> Give us your helping hand
> Do not follow the footprints that make bad tracks along the way
>
> The holy nation belongs to the Most High

---

5. *Uniting in Worship 2*, 218. (I like to add the words "*and help us to forgive*" after the words "forgive us"). Another stunning version of the Lord's Prayer by Jim Cotter begins "Abba, Amma, Beloved." It can be found in Cotter, *Prayer at Night's Approaching*, 36.

The Most High holds us in his hands
The shining greatness of the Most High
Today, yesterday, and forever
That's the way it is!⁶

Each of these versions of the Lord's Prayer slice through the deadening familiarity. In doing so they bring to the surface different elements of Jesus' radical prayer. You may like to experiment with one of these versions of the prayer of resistance, or find others, to explore praying with.

For those who long to connect with the Lord's Prayer in language that is close to the original, but for whom Father language is a barrier, there is another way forward. In seeking to be inclusive and hold space for tradition, I have (re)introduced the language of Aramaic. Thus, the prayer begins: "Our Abba in heaven, hallowed be your name" rather than "Our Father . . . ." The use of the Aramaic connects us directly with the treasured language of the earliest church, as discussed in chapter 2, and creates more room for people to gather to Jesus.

---

6. Champion, *Yarta Wandatha*, 63.

PART TWO: PRAYING IN DAILY LIFE

A Postscript

The suggestions in this chapter may inspire you to explore different ways of praying. Conversely, you may be travelling through a wilderness season that means that these ideas leave you feeling cold. The things is, Christian faith is not a solo event. When we cannot pray, other people can pray for us, and on our behalf, as they did when our babies were in hospital. For people of faith, praying for one another is integral to embodying the kindness of God. In the Uniting Church's liturgy for baptism and for confirmation, the gathered community make this promise to the person:

> With God's help,
> we will live out our baptism
> as a loving community in Christ:
> nurturing one another in faith,
> *upholding one another in prayer,*
> and encouraging one another in service,
> until Christ comes.[7]

Unilateral agreement is not essential in Christian community. Being on the same spiritual plane or doctrinal page is not the primary focus. Instead, *actually* caring about one another is essential, and praying for one another is a core expression of this. When someone among us cannot pray, rather than judging them or being afraid for them, imagine the gift it might be to release them from the burden and guilt of this and instead offer to pray for them. I have witnessed this happening in faith communities. There is power and courage and maturity when someone is able to say "I cannot pray" and others respond by saying "We can do this for you."

---

7. *Uniting in Worship 2*, 83.

Part Three

Praying in the Gathered Community

6
Joining the choirs of angels

CHURCHES, ACROSS DENOMINATIONS, CAN be devastatingly toxic. They can fuel sexism, misogyny, racism, and nationalism. They can be hotbeds of bullying, gossip, and tribalism. They can be bound up in slippery competitive striving to be the nicest or the most self-sacrificing or the angriest social-justice warrior. Churches can be far more loyal to their own constructions of tradition or to their buildings or to a particular genre of music than to the call of the gospel to love. Churches can also be boring. So why show up? In a global context in which, thanks to the internet, vast swathes of the population can access the style of worship that appeals to them on any particular day and endlessly listen to perspectives that reinforce their own views, it is crucial to address this question.

As we explore why people might choose to engage with worship in-person anymore, a wider phenomenon in our society needs to be acknowledged. Increasingly, people are choosing to seek connection online, through watching influencers on social media, scrolling through feeds, or joining online forums, rather than engage with the risks and challenges of physically being in a room with others. However, while popular, evidence is showing that this pattern can lead to greater isolation and ill health, as well as the grooming of extremist views. Just as it is in other spheres of society, this trajectory away from in-person meeting is directly impacting the emerging shape and patterns of religion.

There are certainly online faith communities who foster lively debate and create space for meaningful community for people with a diversity of views. However, such settings can also easily move towards fostering monocultures. When we isolate ourselves from those who think and live differently to us, online or in real life, we run the risk of allowing our brittle edges to calcify. Cynicism about those we disagree with can become our armor—as comfortable as leisure wear and as hard as steel. When we are left to our own devices, our superiority or inferiority complexes are able to flourish in the hot houses of our own heads. When we isolate ourselves, or only associate with those who confirm our own biases, we are susceptible to becoming captive to group think, cults, and conspiracies.

To affirm the value of participating in in-person Christian community is not to pretend that such participation is straightforward. At times people are so wounded by the church that they are no longer able to walk through the door. This is understandable. When we travel through such seasons, particularly when power has been abused, stepping away from the church may be necessary for safety, healing, and for maintaining relationship with the Divine. If you, or those close to you, are in such a season may there be wise companions in the desert who can accompany you, like the angels who waited on Jesus in the wilderness (Mark 1:13).

Amidst the societal movement towards atomization and withdrawal, the answers to the question of why we would bother to show up for worship are urgent, multilayered, and confronting. First, and this is annoying to say, Christianity is a team sport. We need to be together as Christians in order to get free from the idols that dominate each of us. And we need to have intentional room to practice, and fail, and practice again how to love neighbors and enemies in real time, and across all kinds of divides. There is no perfect church. It helps to realize this so that we can stop looking for it, and save our energy. We, and all congregations and denominations, are a mixture of beauty and brokenness.

There is more that is challenging. At their best, church communities will be frustrating. This is because, like the earliest church, they will be made up of contrasts in which rich and poor, young and old, those from different political persuasions and cultural backgrounds, people with diverse abilities, lifestyles, education levels, spiritual maturity, fashion sensibilities, and music tastes are all valued, and try and be kind towards one another. This is hard work. Congregations are called to be places of speaking the truth with love, in which compromise, listening, saying sorry, letting go, and trying again are all part of the DNA. In our increasingly polarized global village, local church communities who seek to live into this call, amidst all their failings, become hubs of resistance to the powers that be.

As we reflect on why we might gather together for worship there is still more to say. Being together for worship is a wild and wonderful waste of time. According to the values of our culture, it does not *do* anything. Instead of labouring to appease the gods of productivity, consumerism, and the attention economy, when we gather together for worship we defy these idols with our very being. We say no. When we come together for worship we testify to the reality that we know that there is more to life. In worship we cleave in body, mind, and spirit to the Triune God who is beyond all our imagining—the enlivening, liberating, and loving One. In gathering for worship in communities in which differences are honored, we defy all those who demand our unquestioning loyalty, whether this be tech-bro billionaires, a world leader, a bullying manager, a toxic family member, or a power-hungry clergyperson. Worship of the Most High is an act of rebellion. If Christ is the Lord, these others are not.

There is even more to say about the potency of worship. The advertising industry continues to tell us that "it is all about us," bombarding us with products that promise to fulfill our every need and bring us to perfection, while simultaneously corroding our sense of worth. Church does not, or *should* not, work like this. We do not sell a product, and we will not fix everything in peoples' lives. Instead, church is a place for honesty and collective *encounter* with God. When we gather together for worship, with all our differences, we are seeking the One who holds us in her tender arms. In church we can stop pretending that everything is #awesome and we can let ourselves breathe out, knowing that others are breathing in and out with us, as they too, with all their wounds, seek the Living One. We do not need to have the shiniest building, the best band or choir, or the happiest or largest congregation. In gathering together, we do not pretend to have everything sorted. Instead, we come together because we are hungry for the Divine. In a world of make believe, one of the greatest gifts we can offer people is authentic, gracious space to name their longings and be met by the Most High.

When a person turns up at church, whether they are an atheist, an agnostic, a seeker, a believer, or just church-curious, they are doing so because they have a hunch that there is more, even though they may not have the words to articulate this. They are responding to something of the presence of the Divine and they want to go deeper. When someone, anyone, bothers to give up their time to attend worship they deserve substance. Anything less is a waste. People do not need second-rate comedy from the front. People do not need worship that is only focused on building community, or reciting words, or sharing a few thoughts. There are plenty of places people can go to be entertained, to find community, or to explore ideas. The one thing that Christians can offer in worship is *serious space for wrestling and communing with the Holy One–Sacred Three. This* is our core business.

In many mainstream churches this priority appears to have been mislaid. We have downplayed, and then forgotten, the critical importance of what we are about. In some settings worship appears to be an exercise in going through the motions. In others, a tone of flippancy and embarrassment has crept into worship. Perhaps this posture stems from the fear that younger people or newcomers won't understand what's going on. Perhaps this emerges in reactive response to the (perceived) fire-and-brimstone church of the past or uncertainty about what we believe anymore. Whatever the reasons, we have lost something. We have, in many places, thrown away the reverence, discarding our strange rhythms and symbols and language, and the power that these have. We have forsaken the beautiful weirdness of Christian faith as we attempt to be accessible. Imagine visiting a Buddhist temple and discovering that all the ancient symbols and practices had been replaced with PowerPoint slides. How would we react? We don't have to be "normal" (there *is* no normal) as people of Christian faith. We are called to be keepers of an ancient story that is alive and shocking and that changes lives.

There *are* ways of honouring our own strangeness and creating ways for people to engage with what is happening and why *and* be able to choose whether to participate or not. Regardless of the denomination or worship style, we need worship that is not diffident, not arrogant, and not busy. We need pauses for *hushedness*, for reverence, so that we can learn together to slow down and open up our hearts to the Living One who is present. In worship we need room to be honest with the Source of all about our gratitude and praise *and* our lament in all the grief and anger. We need to hear from Scripture and have this broken open for us by those who have grappled with these texts prayerfully during the week, engaged with the theological writings of others, *and* have listened to the world. We need space in worship to respond to these words afresh. We need room to be honest about our mistakes and hear a word of hope that the Divine's love is bigger than our own foolishness. In worship we need space to bring our aching for the world, as we pray for justice and mercy and healing. We need room to sing to the Loving One, whether this be songs from the earliest church or those penned this year. In each of these movements we need room to listen for the quiet voice of the Almighty, All-Tender One.

Worship that is interwoven with these components will have gravitas. Gravitas is not the same as dourness or fear mongering. It is worship that takes the task and our lives and the liberative fierce love of the Most High seriously. It is worship that honors that we gather on sacred ground, and this invites us to take off our (metaphorical) shoes—to stop talking and to be alive to the presence of God—even before the opening words of the service are uttered. It is worship that understands that when we sing, we are joining with the choirs of angels, the stars, and the very earth. It is worship that takes seriously that something beyond imagining happened on the third day, and that the Risen One—the One executed by the state, who is infused with a love stronger than death—*is* among us. It is worship that knows that the Spirit is moving with untamed abandon. In order for this kind of worship to exist or flourish, congregations need to ask themselves this critical question: Do we actually trust that God is in the room?

At the beginning

As hinted at above, how we begin worship matters. This is not just in the opening words of the service, but from the moment people walk in the door. Whatever you do, do not express shock or delight if a person under fifty-five arrives with words such as "Oh it is so good to see a young person." Greeting someone like this is a guaranteed way of encouraging them never to return (it is even more dreadful when this kind of welcome is from the lectern). Simply welcome people at the door, young or old, homeless or fancy, a stranger or friend, with openness and respect. Be warm, but give people space. Be confident that they are there because, like you, they sense that there is more to life and they are hoping that your worship community is seeking to create space for that. And, when new people turn up, if in your heart of hearts you worry because the worship makes you cringe, do something. There will be others who feel the same way. It is time to have some hard conversations with the clergy, with Church Council, and with the leadership team about what needs to change.

When I was in placement at Richmond Uniting Church I once used a welcome that was explicitly open, because visitors were expected at the service that day. Afterwards, one of the elders asked if we could have this welcome each week, and so we did. Each week, worship began with someone from the congregation lighting the Christ candle and saying:

You are welcome here. If you are full of faith, or full of doubt, if joy is flowing through you, or sorrow is weighing you down, you are welcome here. Please participate as much or as little as you feel able.

This kind of welcome does two powerful things. First, these words honor that people will be turning up to worship in all kinds of head and heart states—whether they are visitors or members of the congregation. In these opening words, people are assured that there is no pressure to agree, or join in, with whatever unfolds in proclamation, song, symbolic action, or prayer. Secondly, this welcome gives utter freedom to worship leaders and preachers to fully proclaim the hope they have in Christ, without the fear of imposing their convictions upon others.

Prayers of Adoration

In the pages that follow you will find a collection of Calls to Worship and Prayers of Adoration and Praise. They draw from the Psalms and the New Testament for their imagery. These liturgies seek to invite people into the seriousness and the wonder of worship, in ways that are inclusive and expansive. These prayers include silence. If you are presiding, it is worth remembering that it takes courage to hold the space in quiet. At first, collective silence feels awkward and it can be sorely tempting to move on after a few seconds. Developing silence in your own prayer life helps to create space for silence with others, and so too does inwardly praying in the silences during worship (not just saying the prayers and waiting to move on). It also helps to warn people. When I am presiding I often share words, such as those below, before the opening prayer. This kind of explanation could also be printed in an Order of Worship or displayed in the space:

> There is going to be silence in this prayer, and I have not lost my place. It might feel weird because we are not used to being quiet together in our culture. That is ok. Your mind might wander, your tummy might rumble, there might be traffic noises outside. Distractions are normal.

PART THREE: PRAYING IN THE GATHERED COMMUNITY

> Being quiet takes practice. If you find yourself unsettled by the quiet, be gentle with yourself and invite yourself back to this moment. You may like to keep your eyes open or close them, whatever will help you to tune into the Living God. Let us pray . . . .

In the following prayers you will notice that the Triune God is at the heart of things. The calls to worship that accompany each prayer of adoration can be interchanged. Between the call to worship and the prayer, symbolic action such as lighting the Christ candle may be included. In the Australian context, either before worship begins, or after the prayer of adoration, it is the practice in the Uniting Church, and in some other denominations, to have an acknowledgment of country—acknowledging that the lands on which we gather are lands and waterways cared for over millennia by First Nation peoples and that these lands have never been ceded. We also pay our respect to First Nations elders.

Notes on the Prayer of Adoration
"Holy Mystery, Holy Wisdom, Holy Flame"

This prayer draws from the imagery that Jesus uses of the Most High caring for the sparrow (Matt 10:29; Luke 12:22–24; see also Ps 84:3) and the psalmist's imagery of sheltering under the Most High's wings (see for example Ps 57). The language of Jesus calling us to rest is found in Matthew (Matt 11:28). In Matthew 11, Jesus speaks as Woman Wisdom, Sophia.[1] The imagery of the Holy Spirit as fire is drawn from the Pentecost story (Acts 2:1–4). The understanding of the Spirit bringing truth and freedom is drawn from both Romans (Rom 8:14–16) and John's Gospel (John 14:15–17).

---

1. For detailed discussion of Matthew 11, see Douglas, *Jesus Sophia*, 38–40.

PART THREE: PRAYING IN THE GATHERED COMMUNITY

Call to Worship

We are in the presence of the Most High. Let us pray.

Prayer of Adoration and Praise

Holy One–Sacred Three,
Holy Mystery, Holy Wisdom, Holy Flame,
You speak us into being.
So with the stars
we praise you.

Holy Mystery—you care for the sparrow
and call us to find shelter under your wings.
So with the birds
we praise you.

Holy Wisdom—in Jesus
you come among us in person, calling us into rest.
So with the quiet earth
we praise you.

Holy Flame—in Spirit
you awaken us to truth and freedom.
So with wind and fire and skies
we praise you.

JOINING THE CHOIRS OF ANGELS

Holy One–Sacred Three,
Holy Mystery, Holy Wisdom, Holy Flame,
we gather as we are, longing for all that you are:

> *Silence*

In Jesus' sweet name
Amen.

PART THREE: PRAYING IN THE GATHERED COMMUNITY

Notes on the Prayer of Adoration
"Blessed Three: Ground of our being, Water of life, Fire of truth"

The proclamation at the beginning of this prayer is informed by reflections upon trinitarian theology. Within this theology, both the unique Persons *and* the loving Community of the Trinity are honored. To take seriously, not literally, that we are made in the image of the Triune God is, therefore, to recognize that we are each called to be our truest selves *and* to be in community.

The language for the Triune God in this prayer is drawn from both the Psalms and the New Testament. Throughout the Psalms the Most High is referred to as our rock (see Pss 18:1; 28:1; 31:3, etc). In John's Gospel, Jesus offers the water that "will become in them a spring of water gushing up to eternal life" (John 4:14). The Holy Spirit is imaged as fire in Acts (Acts 2:1–4), and is the One who brings truth (see John 14:15–17; Rom 8:14–16).

The language of our restless hearts finding rest in God is from the early church writer Augustine (*Confessions* 1.1.5). The language of worshipping in spirit and in truth is from Jesus' theological conversation with the woman at the well (John 4:23). The alleluia can be said or shouted or sung using a familiar tune. During Lent, the alleluia might be replaced with words such as "holy, holy, holy" or "we adore you."

JOINING THE CHOIRS OF ANGELS

Call to Worship

Let us be still, so that we may become present to the One who is present to us:

Silence

Prayer of Adoration and Praise

Blessed Three:
Ground of our being, Water of life, Fire of truth,
you have made us in your image—
calling us to be ourselves and to be in loving community.
We praise you:
Alleluia, alleluia

You are our source.
You are our rock.
You are our refuge.
We praise you:
Alleluia, alleluia

You bring us home to yourself
by making home with us in Jesus—
the living water.
We praise you:
Alleluia, alleluia

In Spirit you kindle love beyond imagining,
dissolving the lies
and freeing us to take part in your creative reign.
We praise you:
alleluia, alleluia

Blessed Three:
Ground of our being, Water of life, Fire of truth,
our hearts are restless
until they find their rest in you.
So we are still before you.

> *Silence*

May we worship in spirit and in truth this day.
Through Christ we pray. Amen.

Notes on the Prayer of Adoration
"Being of light, Bread of life, Breath of love"

The naming of the Triune God in this prayer is drawn from several places. The title Being of light is inspired by words from the Epistle of James (Jas 1:17) and from a prayer in the *Carmina Gadelica* that refers to God as the "Being of time" and "Being of eternity."[2] The naming of Christ as Bread of life and the Spirit as Breath of love are both drawn from the teaching of the Johannine Jesus (see John 3:8; 6:35).

This Prayer of Adoration also draws from Paul's astonishing words in 2 Corinthians 4:6. First, Paul refers back to the first creation account in which God speaks light into being, and then he proclaims that the same light is illuminating our hearts. Here Paul also speaks of the face of Jesus revealing the knowledge of the glory of God. This is surprising, for Paul has never seen Jesus' face during Jesus' ministry. It may be that Paul's (and perhaps others') ongoing mystical experiences of the risen Jesus inform this profound, collective proclamation.

---

2. De Waal, *The Celtic Vision*, 42.

PART THREE: PRAYING IN THE GATHERED COMMUNITY

Call to Worship

Friends, the Living One welcomes us with outstretched arms.
Let us pray.

Prayer of Adoration and Praise

Being of light, Bread of life, Breath of love,
One God in community,
our beginning and our ending,
we lay down our striving,
we put down our distractions,
we turn to you.

You spoke light into being.
You shine the light of your love in our hearts.
In the face of Jesus we see your glory
and we are nourished into wholeness.
In Spirit you give us new life,
awakening us to your wild compassion

Being of light, Bread of life, Breath of love,
One God in community,
our beginning and our ending:
Hallowed be your name.
With angels and stars and the very earth we say:
Hallowed be your name

> *Silence*

Through Christ Jesus we pray:
May it be so.

Notes on the Prayer of Adoration
"Most High Most Humble"

This prayer holds together language for God from the Psalms (see Ps 91:1) and the conviction that this One chooses to stoop to wash our feet in Jesus (see John 13:1–17). Friends, Christian convictions are astounding!

PART THREE: PRAYING IN THE GATHERED COMMUNITY

Call to Worship

This is sacred time. Let us worship the Triune God.

Prayer of Adoration and Praise

Most High, Most Humble,
you who call each of us by name:
We bless you.

Most High, Most Humble,
you who stoop to wash our feet in Jesus:
We bless you

Most High, Most Humble,
you who in Great Spirit are as close as our breathing:
We bless you.

Your power is embodied in hospitality.
Your love is mightier than evil.
Your grace lavishes and restores us.

We are quiet before you:

Silence

Most High, Most Humble,
all praise be to you, Blessed Three,
now and forever. Amen.

Notes on the Prayer of Adoration
"Almighty, All-Tender Beloved, our God"

The language of Almighty has long been part of Christian worship. However, in many places this naming for God has become deeply problematic because of its connections with empire-shaped thinking (a reality the church has contributed to by its own misuses of power). In naming God as both Almighty and All-Tender, the vastness of God and the shock of the incarnation in the non-retaliatory, living, dying, and resurrected One are held together. The language of "Parent of Good!" is from John Wesley.[3] The imagery of the Spirit as Advocate is from John's Gospel (John 14:15–17).

---

3. Wesley, "Plain Account of Genuine Christianity," secs. 1, 13.

PART THREE: PRAYING IN THE GATHERED COMMUNITY

Call to Worship

God is love, and those who abide in love abide in God, and God abides in them (1 John 4:16).
Let us pray:

Prayer of Adoration and Praise

Almighty, All-Tender,
Beloved, our God,
Three All Holy:
We adore you.

Silence

Parent of Good,
Beloved, our God,
Three All Holy:
We adore you.

Silence

Christ, liberator from evil,
Beloved, our God,
Three All Holy:
We adore you.

Silence

Great Spirit, refiner and advocate,
Beloved, our God,
Three All Holy:
We adore you.

Silence

Almighty, All-Tender,
Beloved, our God,
Three All Holy:
We adore you. Amen.

PART THREE: PRAYING IN THE GATHERED COMMUNITY

Notes on the Prayer of Adoration
"Holy One–Sacred Three, Divine Dance of love"

The language for the Triune God as "Divine Dance of love" is drawn from the Greek term *perichoreses* (*peri*, around + *chōreō*, to go or come), as a way of pointing towards the inner life of the Triune God, flowing in giving and receiving love (see chapter 2 for further discussion).

Call to Worship

The light shines in the darkness, and the darkness did not overcome it (John 1:5). I greet you in the name of the Risen Christ. Let us pray.

Prayer of Adoration and Praise

Holy One–Sacred Three,
Divine Dance of love,
Communion of grace,

we gather amidst our world's pain and beauty,
we gather with our anxieties and questions,
we gather with our joy and our gratitude,

we gather to you as we are,
because you have the words of life,
because you are our restoration.

We lean in together
to this moment,
to your presence.

Silence

We love you.
We worship you.
In Jesus, the radiant One, we pray. Amen.

PART THREE: PRAYING IN THE GATHERED COMMUNITY

Notes on the Prayer of Adoration
"Hidden, Uttered, and Bestowed"

The language of Hidden, Uttered, and Bestowed for naming the Triune God is drawn from the theological writing of Elizabeth Johnson.[4] The language of "Uttered" for Jesus—who is the Word of God—is inspired. In the prayer the description of Jesus "making camp with us" is drawn directly from John 1:14. While the Greek *eskēnōsen* is usually translated as "lived among" or "dwelt," this word literally means "made camp" or "pitched tent."

The prayer also includes a small portion of a responsive psalm. This response could be changed to reflect the psalm set down for any particular Sunday.

---

4. Johnson, *She Who Is*, 215.

Call to Worship

I greet you in the name of the Risen Christ.
Let us worship God.

Prayer of Adoration and Praise

Hidden, Uttered, and Bestowed,
Blessed Trinity,
all glory be to you.

You restore my soul.
You lead me in right paths. (Ps 23:3)

You compose creation.
The rhythms of your grace course through all things
and you long for us to know your life in full.

You restore my soul.
You lead me in right paths. (Ps 23:3)

In Jesus you make camp with us in person,
in compassion that cannot be destroyed,
in light that pierces the night.

You restore my soul.
You lead me in right paths. (Ps 23:3)

PART THREE: PRAYING IN THE GATHERED COMMUNITY

In Spirit Holy you dwell within us,
in power that consumes our fear,
in vital love that makes us new.

You restore my soul.
You lead me in right paths. (Ps 23:3)

Hidden, Uttered, and Bestowed,
Blessed Trinity,
we adore you.

> *Silence*

You restore my soul.
You lead me in right paths. (Ps 23:3)

Through Jesus we pray. Amen.

Notes on the Prayer of Adoration
"Blessed Trinity, our Mother, our Liberator, our Refiner"

While Father language for God is commonplace in Christian worship, Mother language for God continues to be ignored. This is despite the reality that Jesus images himself as a mother in the Gospels (Matt 23:37; Luke 13:34; see also 1 Pet 2:2–3) and God is imaged as a mother in the Old Testament (see, for example, Ps 131; Isa 49:15–16; 66:13). This prayer gives attention to the imagery of God as mother.

The prayer also includes a small portion of a responsive psalm. This response may be changed to reflect the psalm set down for any particular Sunday

PART THREE: PRAYING IN THE GATHERED COMMUNITY

Call to Worship

Jesus says "Come to me all you that are weary . . . and I will give you rest" (Matt 11:28). Let us gather to the Source of Life.

Prayer of Adoration and Praise

Blessed Trinity,
our Mother, our Liberator, our Refiner,

we seek you and your strength,
we seek your presence continually. (Ps 105:4)

Your presence enlightens all life,
creation proclaims your beauty.

We seek you and your strength,
we seek your presence continually. (Ps 105:4)

In Jesus your love is enfleshed,
your kindness and justice greet us in person.

We seek you and your strength,
we seek your presence continually. (Ps 105:4)

In Holy Spirit, you challenge and change us,
emboldening us to share grace and truth.

We seek you and your strength,
we seek your presence continually. (Ps 105:4)

Blessed Trinity,
our Mother, our Liberator, our Refiner,
we are still before you.

Silence

We seek you and your strength,
we seek your presence continually. (Ps 105:4)

In the name of Christ Jesus we pray. Amen.

PART THREE: PRAYING IN THE GATHERED COMMUNITY

Notes on the Prayer of Adoration
"Blessed Trinity Abba, Yeshu, Ruach"

The language of Abba, Yeshu, Ruach offers resonance with the familiar language of Father, Son, and Holy Spirit, in a way that seeks to remain (more) inclusive. As discussed in chapter 2, the language of Abba is Aramaic and means father or dad. This is likely the language Jesus uses to refer to the Most High, and was deeply significant in the earliest church (see Mark 14:36; Rom 8:15; Gal 4:6). Yeshu is from Hebrew, and possibly Aramaic, naming Jesus. Ruach is Hebrew for Spirit, has connections with Aramaic, and also means wind or vital breath.

The imagery of the Ancient of Days is from Daniel (Dan 7:9, 13, 22), and the imagery of Jesus being the bright Morning Star is present both in 2 Peter and in Revelation (2 Pet 1:19; Rev 22:16). The refrain "open the eyes of our hearts" is from a prayer in Ephesians (Eph 1:18). This imagery is also significant in a very early letter from the church in Rome to the church in Corinth (1 Clem. 36.2).

Call to Worship

The Most High is with us.
Let us become present to the One who is present to us. Let us pray.

Prayer of Adoration and Praise

Blessed Trinity,
Abba, Yeshu, Ruach,
we gather to you.
Open the eyes of our hearts.

Ancient of Days,
ceaseless Love,
we gather to you.
Open the eyes of our hearts.

Jesus, bright Morning Star,
disruptive Hope,
we gather to you.
Open the eyes of our hearts.

Spirit of grace,
coursing Freedom,
we gather to you.
Open the eyes of our hearts.

PART THREE: PRAYING IN THE GATHERED COMMUNITY

We slow down our breathing.
We relax our good bodies.
We gather to you.
Open the eyes of our hearts.

Silence

Blessed Trinity,
Abba, Yeshu, Ruach,
with all that we are
we long for all that you are.

Through Jesus the Christ,
amen.

Notes on the Prayer of Adoration
"Holy One–Sacred Three, you cradle the earth in love"

The language of worship and beauty is drawn from the translation in the King James Bible (Ps 96:9). The refrain "holy, holy, holy" may be said or sung or shouted. Instruments, such as bells or shakers, could be used by children (and others) to embody the praise.

PART THREE: PRAYING IN THE GATHERED COMMUNITY

Call to Worship

We gather to the Source of Life. Let us pray.

Prayer of Adoration and Praise

Holy One–Sacred Three,
you cradle the earth in love.
We praise you:
Holy, holy, holy.

Our Parent and Protector,
you sustain all things.
We praise you:
Holy, holy, holy.

In Jesus Sophia
we taste your healing hospitality.
We praise you:
Holy, holy, holy.

In Great Spirit
you birth us into new life.
We praise you:
Holy, holy, holy.

JOINING THE CHOIRS OF ANGELS

Holy One–Sacred Three,
our Source and our Homecoming,
we are still before you.

Silence

May we worship you in the beauty of holiness this day
Amen.

7

Beyond guilt trips

IT IS HARD TO face up to our failings. It is a vulnerable thing to say "I was wrong." It takes courage to say "I am sorry" without diluting the words with excuses or caveats. Across time, drawing from the ancient prayers of the Psalms, Christians have been in the habit of doing this brave work together, saying week by week "we made a mistake." Commonly, these prayers are called Prayers of Confession. However, in more recent years the prayers within this part of the liturgy have become unpopular in some congregations, sometimes leading to their expungement. There are good reasons for reticence about this form of prayer. Too often the language used in confession is at odds with reality. To overly emphasize that we are "unworthy" or "sinners" can veer into denying the goodness of creation, including the goodness of our very own bones and being. When we only emphasize our failings we deny half of the story, ignoring the shocking proclamation in the first creation account that all things, including humanity, are *good* (Gen 1:1—2:3). We also downplay the strange wonder of the gift of the incarnation in which the Divine chooses to embody our good flesh in order to bring us into restorative relationship.

I have no time for church-sponsored guilt trips in worship. However, the gift of being able to face the truth within ourselves, in our churches, and in our global village is too precious to simply discard. Prayers of Confession can be strong enough to hold our complex truths, courageously naming the paradoxical realities that we inhabit: we are made in the image of God and are good *and* we are often grasping, defensive, and self-seeking, hurting one another and ourselves. Both these things are true at the same time. They do not cancel one another out. In our prayers in worship, we need space to hold together both our beauty and belovedness *and* our entanglements with fear and violence as we seek the Divine's healing grace.

Not only is the traditional language for Prayers of Confession often one-sided in its focus upon sinfulness, these prayers can also be largely irrelevant for half of the population. In patriarchal contexts, cultural conditioning encourages men to be motivated by pride and greed, often rewarding men for domineering behavior. With few exceptions, this is not the case for women. Women are conditioned by patriarchal cultures to wear shame like a garment and to endlessly give themselves away. While there are women who are dominating and ego-driven, for many women "sin" is not manifest in pride, but instead, is bound up in self-loathing and a lack of self-care or boundaries. Despite this reality, Prayers of Confession, written predominantly by men over millennia, continue to focus on pride and selfishness as *key* expressions of sin. This is not sufficiently honest. We need prayers that can speak into the breadth of being, and the myriad ways in which we all fall short of love.

Jesus' great call for living, found across the Synoptic Gospels, involves three movements. We are called to love God with our whole being, to love our neighbors, *and* we are called to love ourselves (see Matt 22:34-40; Mark 12:28-34; Luke 10:25-28). Note, it is not possible to genuinely love others if we do not care for and have regard for ourselves, as we only become embittered or self-righteous. At any given time in our lives, we will tend to be stronger in one of these three spheres of love, and weaker in the others. At times we may be good at loving our neighbors but ignore self-care. At times we will be great at tuning into God, but forget about supporting those in need around us. Or we may be so busy doing good for others, or pursuing our own path, that we entirely ignore God's presence in our lives and in the process become

PART THREE: PRAYING IN THE GATHERED COMMUNITY

annoying mini-messiahs. We can find ourselves emphasizing one of these spheres to the detriment of the others in different seasons of our lives, or this can occur over the course of a week or in a day. At the heart of things, whether we become lopsided because of our self-abnegation or self-obsession, we are relentlessly called back to the center so that we may experience wholeness and healing. The Living One longs to set us free—now—to haul us into balance so that we may dwell in the middle of the Divine Dance of love for all things, including us.

This is where a practice of Prayers of Confession can be profound. Rather than a collective guilt trip in which we are expected to hunt out our faults and grovel in the dirt, this pattern of prayer can be an opportunity to get real—to finally be honest with ourselves about what is happening within ourselves, within our churches, and across our global village. It is a free gift in which we can stop pretending that it is all ok and acknowledge that we have fallen short of how we had hoped to live and are out of sync. Despite the terrible ways in which these prayers are often shared, Prayers of Confession can be liberating. In engaging with this ongoing gift in communal worship, those who construe themselves as shameful can learn to put down their self-loathing and experience healing. And those who think that they are superior to others can experience Christ's excoriating truth and be liberated from their deceptions. In these prayers we have the opportunity to name our own failings, the church's mistakes, and the systemic violence that corrupts our world. However, the acknowledgement of our failings is not all that happens in these prayers.

In Prayers of Confession, acknowledging our mistakes—putting down our heavy guilt and all the stories we rehearse about our ourselves—is only the first movement. In the Declaration of Forgiveness we hear about life beyond our own toxicity. At the end of this prayer that helps us to tell the truth, we are told that there is hope. It is not all up to us. Within the Protestant tradition in which I stand, we proclaim the conviction that Christ is the one who forgives, and no human intermediary is necessary. In the Declaration of Forgiveness we *each* hear, both worship leaders and congregants, Christ's word of grace: "Your sins are forgiven." In this moment of raw truth-telling we are greeted with tenderness and called to let hope settle in our hearts. We are called out of despair by the One who brings life out death, who meets us and is able to restore us, and grow us up in love. To have the courage to collectively admit our faults and to receive Christ's word of grace is to dwell at the frontier of transformation.

Prayers of Letting Go

We do not need to remove Prayers of Confession from the liturgy in order to avoid mechanized guilt trips. There are ways of honoring the gift of this tradition that bring life. One way forward is to attend to the language that we use, not only in the content of the prayers but also in the name we give to these prayers. At its best, worship will always be prayerfully prepared with an ear to how it will sound to someone turning up for the first time. This is an evangelical imperative. For many people, both those who have attended worship in the past and those who have never been to church, a word like "confession" is alien. In contemporary life such language is often associated with the courtroom or splashy articles about public figures admitting their gross misconduct. Turning up to worship for the first time and being asked to "confess" will be a hindrance to many people. In response to this, I created the language of "Prayers of Letting Go." I regularly introduce this part of the liturgy with words such as the following. Equally, words like this could be included in the Order of Worship:

> The word *aphesis* "forgiveness" in the Greek of the New Testament literally means "let go" or "release." The same word is used for releasing a captive or a prisoner. This ancient pattern of prayer in the church is not a guilt trip, but a rare gift that enables us to be honest with ourselves and the Source of all about what is pinning us down and blocking love, and to seek release.

For both visitors and regular church attendees this knowledge can be a powerful way of carving out space to be open to this counter-cultural practice. Another way of describing this part of the liturgy is "Prayers of Liberation." Within discussions in your community, you might create new language.

The placement of these prayers within the liturgy varies across the worldwide church. In many congregations, these prayers, if included, come directly after the Prayers of Adoration and Praise or are woven into them. The solid argument for this placement is linked with coming before God's majesty and acknowledging our littleness and mistakes. However, there are reasons, both evangelical and theological, for placing these prayers later in the service. If we think about how we express the good news within the shape of the liturgy, often it is too soon in the service, especially for new people, to be plunged into thinking about their faults. People need time to settle into their seat and to begin to let their hearts beat in time with the strange rhythms of worship. There is more at stake. From a theological perspective, often we do not know what our truth is—how love is being blocked in our lives and church and society—until we have heard from Sacred Scripture and had this broken open for us in preaching, or other forms of proclamation. While there are sound arguments for having Prayers of Letting Go near the beginning of worship, often these prayers are better placed after the proclamation and a time of silence for personal reflection.

A final note about this prayer practice. In consumerist culture, which emphasizes the importance of the individual, it is crucial that we remember that these prayers are for the gathered community and our world. While we may have much to become honest about in our personal lives as we seek the Divine's cleansing and healing, these prayers also offer space for bringing our collective guilt before God. The human family has much to acknowledge about our misuse of the planet, the horrendous discrepancies in wealth and poverty that dominate our global village, and countless other travesties. Admitting our communal failings and *together* receiving the declaration of the Risen Christ's liberation is powerful.

Here, no longer pinned down by despair, we are emboldened to live in prophetic ways as faith communities.

In the Prayers of Letting Go below you will find examples that focus on systemic sin and on personal failings. The words of assurance are drawn from the biblical text and can be used interchangeably. The biblical basis for the bulk of the imagery found in these prayers has been discussed in previous chapters and may be referred to again. In the first prayer, the wild imagery of the Source of all knowing the hairs on our heads and caring about us is found in Luke (Luke 12:7).

In the pages that follow there are occasional notes before some prayers, particularly as these relate to symbolic action.

PART THREE: PRAYING IN THE GATHERED COMMUNITY

Prayers of Letting Go

Love at the heart of the universe,
you who count the hairs on our heads,
your compassion becomes personal in Jesus.

You call us to dwell in grace and truth as you do—
loving you, and loving neighbor, and loving ourselves—
and you know where it hurts right now.

You know where love is blocked between us and within us—
where fear is pinning us down.
In the silence we tell you our truth.

> *Silence*

Set us free by your risen life,
revive our beings with your Being,
through Jesus, whose love is stronger than death, we pray. Amen.

Words of Assurance and Declaration of Christ's Forgiveness

"Christ has forgiven us. Therefore let us be imitators of God, as beloved children, and live in love as Christ loved us." (Eph 5:1–2a)

Friends, hear these words of Jesus to each one of us and let them sink into our hearts:
"Your sins are forgiven."
Thanks be to God.

Prayers of Letting Go

Holy Mystery, Holy Wisdom, Holy Flame,
One God in community,
we are made in your image
to give love and to receive love.

Liberate us from the lies of isolation,
save us from our messiah complexes,
rescue us from the violence of consumerism,
so that we, and the whole earth, may find our freedom and balance
in you.

> *Silence*

Through Christ Jesus—face of God among us—we pray. Amen.

Words of Assurance and Declaration of Christ's Forgiveness

"God was in Christ reconciling the world to God's self, not counting our trespasses against us, and entrusting to us the message of reconciliation." (2 Cor 5:19)

Friends, hear Christ's word of grace to every single one of us: "Your sins are forgiven."
Thanks be to God.

Prayers of Letting Go

Almighty, All-tender God, our beginning and our ending,
you cry out for justice,
you bless the peacemakers,
you embody the way of true life in Jesus' fierce compassion.
In our society, in the church, and in our lives we have fallen short
of your dreamings.

We have confused being loving with being nice.
We have resisted hard conversations, afraid to speak the truth.
We have allowed evil to flourish because it is easier to go with the
flow.
We have fallen into the trap of despair.
Set us free.

   Silence

In Jesus' risen life, the lies of violence are dissolved.
In Jesus' risen life, the chains of fear are broken.
In Jesus' risen life, we taste your love that is stronger than hate.
Nourish us now by your power
so that we may play our part in your symphony of grace for all
things. Amen.

Words of Assurance and Declaration of Christ's Forgiveness

"God is love. . . . There is no fear in love, but perfect love casts out fear." (1 John 4:16, 18)

Friends, this is Christ's word of grace to every single one of us—listen:
"Your sins are forgiven."
Thanks be to God.

PART THREE: PRAYING IN THE GATHERED COMMUNITY

Notes about the Prayer of Letting Go
"Blessed Trinity, you come to us in Jesus, the fragrance of grace"

This prayer, which draws from 2 Corinthians 2:14–16, includes an invitation to engage with symbolic action. Before worship begins, place a bowl of water with river pebbles around it, on a small table in the middle of the worship space, or place these things near or on the Communion table as appropriate. You may like to light an oil burner before worship, so that fragrances such as orange or frankincense (non-headache-inducing scents) can infuse the worship space during worship.

The symbolic action of inviting people to wash a stone and place this around the Christ candle is inspired by Judith Hall's book focused on creating meaningful and participatory worship for children. Within her book, Hall suggests the liturgical action of using stones, ash, water, and the Christ candle.[1]

I continue to witness both young and old people relishing the opportunity to engage with prayer in action rather than words. It may help to ease any awkwardness by having quiet music on in the background for this time of prayer, particularly so that people don't feel pressure to rush.

---

1. Hall, *In Their Midst*, 63–67.

Prayers of Letting Go

Blessed Trinity,
you come to us in Jesus, the fragrance of grace,
calling us into your overflowing compassion for all things.
You know where the stench of fear and death, hate and despair
pervade our lives, our families, our churches, and our world.

In the power of Great Spirit cleanse us,
wash us out,
cascade through us—
birthing your love and renewing to us the joy of your salvation:

> *In silence, or with quiet music in the background, people may choose a river stone, wash it in the bowl of water, and place this stone around the Christ candle*

In Christ, yours is the victory of love. Amen.

Words of Assurance and Declaration of Christ's Forgiveness

"In Christ all the fullness of God was pleased to dwell and through Christ, God was pleased to reconcile all things." (Col 1:19–20)

Friends, may Christ's word of hope grow within us:
"Your sins are forgiven."
Thanks be to God

PART THREE: PRAYING IN THE GATHERED COMMUNITY

Prayers of Letting Go

Holy One–Sacred Three,
you call us to *be* in love
and to use our power for others.

You know what is holding us back.
You know what is blocking our love for you, for others, and for ourselves.
In the silence we tell you our truth:

> *Silence*

Break through the barricades,
rescue us from our delusions,
so that we may walk forward with you in your wild compassion.

Through Christ Jesus, our liberator, we pray. Amen.

Words of Assurance and Declaration of Christ's Forgiveness

"We have this hope, a sure and steadfast anchor of the soul." (Heb 6:19)

Friends, Christ, our freedom and anchor, says to each of us:
"Your sins are forgiven"
Thanks be to God

Notes about the Prayers of Letting Go
"Precious Christ, Bread of life"

Following this prayer, there is an invitation (this should never be compulsory) for people to come forward to receive anointing in the name of Christ. While this is an ancient Christian practice (see Jas 5:14), it has dropped out of many denominations. Having the symbolic action of receiving oil for anointing can be deeply impactful. It may be placed after any of the Prayers of Letting Go and may be accompanied by the quiet singing of a chant or refrain or instrumental music. Prepare a little bowl of olive oil before worship and have this near the Christ candle, ready to hold in the middle of the worship space for those who come forward.

PART THREE: PRAYING IN THE GATHERED COMMUNITY

Prayers of Letting Go

Precious Christ, Bread of life,
we come to you in our hunger.
We are starving for you—for your energy, wisdom, and courage.
We are aching for the freedom to let things go that are not love—
in our global village, in our churches, and in our being.
We are honest with you about the places where we have nothing.

Silence

Risen Jesus, Bread of life,
nourish us into wholeness;
bless us, that we may be blessing to others. Amen.

Words of Assurance and Declaration of Christ's Forgiveness

"Nor height, nor depth, nor anything else in all creation will be able to separate us from the love of God in Christ Jesus our Lord." (Rom 8:39)

Friends, this is Christ's loving word of grace to every single one of us:
"Your sins are forgiven."
Thanks be to God

Invitation to Receive Anointing

If people choose to come forward, mark the sign of the cross on their forehead (or hand if they prefer) and pray with words such as:

(*name*) I anoint you in the name of Christ Jesus for healing and wholeness.

Prayers of Letting Go

Holy One–Sacred Three,
Our Fortress, our Friend, and the Fire within our bones,
you come to us in Jesus embodying love;
in Spirit, you ignite us with your truth and grace.

When we are too afraid to speak up or challenge,
please love us into change.

When we are stuck in despair or arrogance,
please love us into change.

When we seek to dominate others or dismiss ourselves,
please love us into change.

Silence

Through Jesus, we pray. Amen.

Words of Assurance and Declaration of Christ's Forgiveness

Friends, we are called to dwell and be in love. Be assured, for God all things are possible (Matt 19:26).

So hear and receive Christ's word of grace to each one of us:
"Your sins are forgiven"
Thanks be to God

Notes about Prayers of Letting Go
"Blessed Three, you who name the stars"

This prayer was originally written for the Uniting Church Assembly's Uniting in Prayer Project (2024). The focus of the prayer is acknowledging the ways in which the church limits the wild love of God. The imagery of fire burning away anxiety and that which is dead is inspired by the wisdom of Indigenous Fire-stick burning practices. The words of the stanza after the silence are drawn from Wesley's Covenant prayer. The language of enjoying the Holy One is drawn from the Westminster Shorter Catechism.

PART THREE: PRAYING IN THE GATHERED COMMUNITY

Prayers of Letting Go

Blessed Three,
you who name the stars,
you who make camp with us in Jesus,
you who renew us in Spirit,
O God, our restoration,
we praise you.

For the love glimpsed across your church
as we are befriended by you and make friends with others—
    feasting with the hungry,
    advocating for justice,
    journeying with the broken-hearted
—strengthen us.

From the fear that poisons your church
when stories of scarcity replace listening for you—
    buildings becoming idols,
    self-preservation consuming our energy,
    despair suffocating hope
—rescue us.

Ancient of Days clothed in mystery, light, and fire,
thaw out our hearts,
kindle your wild grace,
burn away the anxiety and all that is dead within us,
so that your love and joy and peace may grow
and we may dream your dreams.

Silence

Put us to what you will.
Rank us with whom you will.
Let us have all things, let us have nothing.
Awaken us to the scent of the kingdom here and now
so that even when we do not know the way
we dare to enjoy walking with you, the Way.

Blessed Three,
our Rock, our Liberator, our Refiner,
you who bring life out of death,
O God, our restoration,
take our hand, lead us forward, make us brave,
through Jesus we pray. Amen.

Words of Assurance and Declaration of Christ's Forgiveness

"In Christ all the fullness of God was pleased to dwell and, through Christ, God was pleased to reconcile all things." (see Col 1:19–20)

Friends, hear Christ's word of reconciling grace to all of us:
"Your sins are forgiven"
Thanks be to God

PART THREE: PRAYING IN THE GATHERED COMMUNITY

A note about responses after Bible readings

Regardless of whether the Prayers of Letting Go are placed before or after the readings from the biblical text, the words that are used when the Bible is read matter. In many churches, after a portion from the biblical text is read, the reader says, "This is the word of the Lord" and the congregation responds, "Thanks be to God." While common, this is deeply problematic. From the earliest church, Jesus followers have made the most remarkable claim, and it is far bigger than this. For Christians, our religion is not centred on a book or set of laws. From the outset, Christians have claimed that in the person of Jesus we behold the Divine. Jesus is the One at the center, in whom "the whole the fullness of the deity dwells bodily" (Col 2:9). For Christians, *Jesus*—not a book—is the Word of God. This is what the Johannine prologue proclaims (John 1:1).

When we minimize the radical nature of our faith, claiming that the Bible, and not Jesus—the incarnate, living, dying, and risen One—is the Word of God, we run the risk of heresy. We also run the risk of misusing the Bible. When people insist that the Bible is the word of God, then its contradictions must be denied and its complexity must be papered over. If the Bible is the word of God, then we can slice out our favorite quotes in order to bolster our own arguments, pretending that our views are divine. As followers of Jesus, we are tasked with much harder work. We are called to love God with our mind (see Matt 22:37; Mark 12:30; Luke 10:27) and, therefore, to engage seriously and faithfully with the complexity and contradictions of the biblical text, as we seek to hear the Word of God, Jesus the Christ, within it.

This distinction cannot be overstated. For Christians, Jesus is the lens—the window—through which we read our sacred text. Jesus, who according to the Gospels consistently welcomes and teaches, forgives and heals, challenges and feeds. Jesus, who rejects retaliating with violence and who instead endures our violence even to death. Jesus, whose love could not be held down by the grave and whose risen life breathed out peace, *is* the Word of God. Any passage within our sacred text must therefore be read *through*

Jesus the Christ, the Holy Human One, who is the Word made flesh. For this reason, the early church theologian Augustine wrote the following instructions about how to read the Bible:

> So anyone who thinks that he has understood the scriptures, or any part of them, but cannot by his understanding build up this double love of God and neighbor, has not yet succeeded in understanding them. (*On Christian Doctrine*, 1.36.40)

Because of the wild conviction that Jesus is the Word of God, when we come to passages within the biblical text that appear to call for violence or to justify hate, if we are Christians we have to read these words *through* Jesus, the One who embodies and calls us into radical compassion for all.

While the Bible is not the word of God for us, the Bible cannot be replaced. As the Uniting Church's *Basis of Union* proclaims with deft insight, "the church has received the books of the Old and New Testaments as *unique, prophetic, and apostolic testimony* in which it hears the Word of God" (Para 5). Here, within these sacred texts, we hear the Word speaking. However, for many people in congregations these crucial distinctions between Jesus the Word and the biblical text are not clear. The ongoing habit of saying "This is the word of God" after Bible readings makes this difficult situation worse.

In response to this issue, some congregations utilize language from the Psalms and Gospels before and after readings. For example:

> Your word is a lamp to my feet
> **And a light to my path** (Ps 119:105)

and

> May your word live in us
> **And bear much fruit to your glory** (see John 15:5)

This language is beautiful but, without ongoing teaching, does not disrupt the assumption that the biblical text is the word of God. In seeking to attend to this dilemma, I created the following response that holds the tension of our faith:

> For these words of faith and Jesus the Word
> **Thanks be to God**

Another congregation adapted these words to the following:

> For these words of witness and Christ the Word
> **Thanks be to God**

Both these responses offer a way forward in holding open the complex way in which the church honors sacred text *and* the One at the heart of our faith, the Word made flesh. Perhaps these responses will prompt discussions and fresh creativity in your own worship contexts.

8

Praying for others?

In the song "Into My Arms" by Nick Cave and the Bad Seeds, released in 1997, Cave croons about rejecting the idea of a God who intervenes. While this song continues to be an anthem for many, in more recent years, in a highly unfashionable turn for a rock icon, Nick Cave's writing and music have begun engaging with questions of God, transcendence, mystery, and suffering.[1] Ideas about God intervening, or not, often hinge on images of God that look a lot like a (male) puppet master. The working logic underneath this kind of construction appears to be that in the face of suffering, if God is powerful, then God should swoop in to fix things, and if God doesn't, God must be powerless to act, non-interventionist, or non-existent.

When we endure grave suffering, especially when it is unexpected, we crave a logical way of making the absurdity comprehensible. We long for there to be a reason for the chaos, so that out of the obliterated pieces of what we thought our life would be, we can cobble together a coherent story. When people are flung to the edge of the abyss, and stuck in the binary of assuming that God is either a superhero or powerless, it is understandable that

---

1. See Nick Cave's ongoing reflections as he responds to peoples' letters asking about death, life, grief, God, and the universe: Red Hand Files (https://www.theredhandfiles.com). Recent albums by Nick Cave include *Carnage* with Warren Ellis (2021), *Seven Psalms* (2022), and *Wild God* (2024) with Nick Cave and the Bad Seeds.

PART THREE: PRAYING IN THE GATHERED COMMUNITY

particular "answers" come to dominate. For some, this is expressed in the atheistic conviction that God does not exist. For others, the answer is supplied through contemporary renditions of karma such as "I chose this suffering for my soul" or "everything happens for a reason."

When Christians are faced with unexpected suffering, this kind of thinking is also present. In order to maintain space for the existence of God, Christians might supplement such thinking by turning to blame themselves for God's perceived inactivity with ideas such as "I am being punished," or "God is testing me," or "I didn't pray hard enough." While for people of Christian faith, and for people who claim no faith, these kinds of responses are ways of seeking to claim control in chaotic times, these "answers" do damage to us. This is because they are born of desperation and are not grounded in the truth. Control is seductive. However, allowing ourselves to acknowledge the chaos, stay with our raw grief, and wrestle with the reality that we do not know why this suffering is happening, gives us space to finally be real and be met by the Divine—in the mess—just as the psalmists do.

In the church if we are going to engage with the age-old task of praying for others, we need to be able to talk about why we would do this, how this relates to God and God's power, and how we understand God to act (or not) when we pray. These conversations do not appear to happen very much in mainstream churches. We have become reticent to talk about why we would pray for others and whether we think anything comes of intercessory prayer. This is a significant issue. In refusing to create space for these hard conversations, people are left with their fear and shame, and the kinds of deeply problematic "answers" described above when terrible things happen.

The ambiguity and doubt that many Christians have about what praying for others achieves not only has significant pastoral consequences but has also contributed to new contours within worship. Increasingly in churches that are not bound by prayer books, intercessory prayers often resemble the "shopping list of doom" introduced in chapter 1. Recent global tragedies are listed,

PRAYING FOR OTHERS?

as though God might not have heard about these events during the week and it is the responsibility of a church member to inform the Divine. It is not uncommon for these prayers, or inventories of tragedy, to consist of "remembering" situations. For example, "Lord, we remember the people of Sudan," while offering no actual prayer for change. Does it really make a difference if we remember? Are we only remembering and naming tragic situations in order to appear righteous and informed, while concurrently feeling guilty about living in a relatively peaceful situation? Is this actually prayer? What might it mean to bring particular situations in our global village to God and expect the Heart of the universe to respond in love?

In order to address this question, the construction of the interventionist God needs to be interrogated. This is because this idea of God has little to do with Christianity. It is a false dichotomy to think that we need to choose sides on a seesaw between either believing that God intervenes like an omnipotent puppet master or assuming that God is impotent or imaginary. If it is true, that in some serious way, Jesus is the Word of God, the Divine with skin on, then we need to attend to *how* Jesus embodies power across the Gospels in order to recognize the *texture* of divine power in our lives and the world. In Jesus we are confronted with the God One who chooses to use power *for* others, and not *over* others. Suffering is not avoided by this One. Instead, knowing our proclivity for violence, Jesus keeps speaking and being love, even when this leads to betrayal, arrest, corrupt trial, beatings, and execution. What is more, Jesus keeps on loving like this right through the other side.

The male disciples are not expecting this. Peter's response to Jesus' frankness about the reality that he will be betrayed and suffer makes this clear (see Mark 8:31–33). These disciples want power and glory according to human standards, including front-row seats when Jesus is established as the true king (as reflected in the request of James and John, and the anger of the others, see Mark 10:35–41). Instead of happy endings, honor, and political glory, Jesus endures breathtaking humiliation. Jesus does not get down from the cross. Jesus did not magic away the pain or smite the enemies. Jesus is killed in a state-sanctioned murder, executed as a threat to the empire in agony and desolation. If Jesus is Emmanuel, God-with-us, then divine power looks very different to human ideas of power. This is exactly what Paul states when he writes to the church in Corinth, whose members are struggling to make sense of, and are embarrassed by, Jesus' crucifixion (see 1 Cor 1:21–25).

Despite all the movies, the artwork, and the archetypes, can our ideas of divine power be changed in the light of Jesus? For Christians, if Jesus is the God One, then our understandings of divine power must correlate with the shape of *who and how* Jesus embodies power within the Gospels, and the wider testimony of the New Testament. We do not have the false luxury of a Zeus God who is all controlling and smashing enemies. We cannot pretend that God is like a fairy godmother who alleviates problems and magics away the pain with a flick of a wand. The God of Jesus Christ walks *into our suffering* to endure this with us. According to the testimony of the Gospels, divine power—as embodied by Jesus—is expressed in a *bearing with* love that refuses to impose itself. Paul tells about this divine love like this:

> Love is patient; love is kind; love is not envious or boastful or arrogant or rude. It does not insist on its own way; it is not irritable or resentful; it does not rejoice in wrongdoing, but rejoices in the truth. It *bears all things, believes all things, hopes all things, endures all things.* (1 Cor 13:4–7)

The God of Christian faith is nothing like the superheroes and puppet masters of our imagination and nightmares. These are fake, plastic parodies of true power.

It is astonishing that we, in the church, keep missing this. Not only does Jesus embody this *bearing with* love-as-power, Jesus talks openly about how divine power—the kingdom way—looks utterly different to human ideas of power. Repeatedly utilizing metaphors, Jesus speaks of the Divine's unpower.[2] Jesus says that divine power

---

2. I coined the phrase "unpower" due to the limitations of English. Powerless is not an adequate term to describe the kind of power that Jesus embodies and teaches about. This is because Jesus *does* have power across the Gospels,

is like a crop mysteriously growing unseen overnight (see Mark 4:26–29). Jesus says divine power is like a tiny seed growing into a bush that gives shade to the birds (see Mark 4:30–32). Jesus says divine power is like a woman who keeps on searching for that which is lost, celebrating when she finds it (Luke 15:8–10). Can we actually imagine that God's power, divine power, the reign of God, is like this, not simply as an abstract concept, but vital and moving *within* the fabric of our own lives and the world?

Jesus' *bearing with* death is not the end of the story. The victory of divine love is proclaimed on Easter Day. However, the risen life that emerges on Easter Day is still not what the disciples are expecting. This victory does not inaugurate the longed-for political uprising, the expulsion of the occupiers, or the eradication of pain. While there continue to be miracles through the power of the risen Christ, as reflected in Acts (e.g., Acts 5:14–16; 9:32–35; 20:7–12), this victory does *not* take away all suffering, injustice, or conflict. This is graphically reflected both in Acts (e.g., Acts 7:54–60; 12:1–5; 19:23–41; 27:39–44), and in Paul's own letters (e.g., 2 Cor 11:23–28; Gal 2:11–14; 5:11–15; 1 Thess 1:6; 2:14–15).

In contrast to hopes and expectations, this victory of love is witnessed in the transforming of tiny groups of Jesus followers—who are still often fighting and afraid. Together they are being changed. Little communities are experiencing unheard of and unimagined homecoming and wholeness, and being empowered to live in extraordinarily different ways because of this. They are (falteringly) becoming more like Jesus. Through the ongoing presence of the risen, crucified One and the verdancy of the Spirit's power within and among them, they are becoming kinder, more hopeful, and are tasting joy and experiencing a deep-down peace (e.g., Rom 8:9–21; Gal 5:22–25). Despite ongoing ridicule, hatred, illnesses, unexpected sorrows, and, for some, persecution, people in Jesus communities are experiencing a love that is stronger than fear in the marrow of their beings. What is more, they are sharing

---

but chooses to use this power in ways that are in radical contrast to the powers of patriarchy and empire. For further reading, see my article "The Problem with Powerlessness."

PART THREE: PRAYING IN THE GATHERED COMMUNITY

this love generously with those beyond their own communities who are sick, poor, or vulnerable, as well as with those they had been taught to hate and those who hate them. As a result, people around them are noticing and begin to be changed (see Justin Martyr, *1 Apol.* 14). *This* is the architecture of the victory of divine love. *This* is what the heartbeat of divine power sounds like. Yes, Jesus the God One changes the world, but not in the ways the first disciples, and often we too, expect.

Like those in the earliest church, we are invited to be transformed by the same strange unpower. We are not going to avoid suffering. Faith is not an insurance policy against bad things happening. It is not going to be easy. Jesus is completely honest about this (see Matt 16:21–26; Mark 8:31–38; Luke 9:21–26). Divine power does not impose solutions, smash people, or magic all suffering away, but *bears with* the pain and weaves the good from within this. This is power that kindles the kind of ferocious compassion that speaks truth to evil, that extends kindness, and that carries the scent of hope and beauty into places that reek of death and hate. Within Jesus' living, dying, rising, and ongoing presence we are confronted with divine power that looks nothing like patriarchal and empire-shaped constructions of power. If we take this seriously, how might we pray?

For as long as we are fixated on action movie or puppet master imagery for God, we will miss what the Divine is doing, or secretly succumb to the fear that God is dead. We need to learn to look at the world, and our lives, through the lens of how Jesus exudes divine power and pray accordingly. This takes time. It takes practice to focus our eyes and begin to recognize that the movement of God, the kingdom's ways, are often little, relational, unexpected, and half-seen, just as Jesus talks about in the kingdom parables. Sometimes this is witnessed in the emergence of a creative solution, the hatching of a new way forward when a situation is completely stuck. Sometimes the words of a stranger burst through with clarity about an issue that has been weighing us down, even though the stranger has no idea about this. Sometimes this movement of divine love is experienced when someone unexpectedly enters into your life with friendship, wisdom, and support in a dire moment. Sometimes this is witnessed in unexpected healing or feasting, or new beginnings, in peoples' lives, relationships, or communities. Sometimes there is release from the grip of the past, or fresh courage to work for justice. Sometimes we see the kingdom at work in (so called) coincidences.

I wonder if these signposts pointing to the unpower of the Divine resonate with your own experiences? In my own life, most of these kinds of unexpected happenings have *only* emerged when I have finally stopped trying to fix the problem and flung myself into the arms of the Divine crying, "Help!" When we are trying to be our own messiahs, we leave little room for God. When we surrender this facade, then the table-turning and the weaving of the unexpected beauty can begin. While pivotal and transformational, these kinds of experiences of divine unpower will probably not make the headlines, nor do they fix everything. Yet, the Spirit *is* at work, blowing where she will, bearing new life into toxic places within us and around us, if only we look (John 3:3, 7–8). Life is still loaded with challenges and struggles; pain is not vacuum-sucked from a Christian's day. However, the Source of all is moving and steadfastly laboring for restoration and freedom—for me, for you, and for all things. There is power, or rather unpower, in her wings.

As we think about the dynamic unpower of God and prayer, there is another question that we need to address. From Christian perspective, how much power does God have and how much freedom do we have in our lives? This is a conundrum that will continue to fill many, many volumes. Here, in response to this question, I invite us to briefly turn again to the story of Jesus that is woven through several of the liturgies in this book. In both Luke and Matthew's Gospels, Jesus likens himself to a mother hen, who longs to gather Jerusalem under her wings. Alongside the reality that here Jesus images himself as the female divine,[3] what is striking is that while Jesus expresses longing to gather up the people, the people have *refused* to be embraced:

---

3. For discussion, see Douglas, *Jesus Sophia*, 40–41.

PART THREE: PRAYING IN THE GATHERED COMMUNITY

> How often have I desired to gather your children together as a hen gathers her brood under wings, and you were not willing! (Matt 23:37; cf. Luke 13:34)

Each of these accounts points to the reality that the Divine respects our choice. God does not impose healing, does not enforce change, and does not demand reconciliation. This diverges wildly from the kinds of images of God in popular culture, and from the pantheon of Greek and Roman gods dominating at the time these texts were composed. Here, and as reflected throughout Jesus' ministry in the Gospels, people have power. Despite the common misconceptions, this reality coalesces with the imagery of the Divine in the Old Testament. Again and again we hear from the prophets about how the Most High longs to gather up the people, yet they refuse, and God grieves (e.g., Jer 2:4–13). When Jesus laments over Jerusalem's refusal to be reconciled, this emerges from within this tradition.

In the Gospels, Jesus does not chase after people, vaporize them, or harangue them about being healed or reconciled. Instead, people consistently choose to come to Jesus, and when they do, Jesus asks people what they want, and listens, and responds. Jesus' question "do you want to be made well?" (see John 5:6) is open and ongoing for each of us. If Jesus *is* actually "the image of the invisible God" (Col 1:15), Emmanuel, God-with-us (Matt 1:23), the Word made flesh (John 1:1), then we are faced with something confronting. We have power in our relationship with God, to receive grace or to walk away, to seek healing or to close ourselves off from it. And so does everyone else.

As we reflect upon divine unpower—upon the God who bears all things, wading into our pain to heal us, waiting for each of us to say yes—it becomes clear that the internal dynamics of Christian prayer cannot be translated into transactional formulas such as "pray this and get that." There are no vending machines in Christian faith. There are no divine bulldozers or army tanks. Instead, we are each invited into intimate, dynamic relationship. In Jesus the Christ we see that the Divine works in the personal, one-to-one. Jesus meets each person as they are, truly seeing them

PRAYING FOR OTHERS?

and loving them, and inviting them into transformation (see Mark 10:21).

Recognizing the one-to-one nature of divine power has implications, not only for our individual lives but also for how we are called to pray for others. Instead of praying generically for whole countries, vaguely hoping that things get better, we are called to pray for creative ways forward for specific people within particular situations. Rather than offering wishes for fairytale solutions, imagine praying for specific outcomes in line with Gospel values. We might pray for the UN representatives at a certain meeting or key leaders from warring factions to be moved to work towards peace and justice. We might pray for volunteers at soup kitchens to be sustained in their work, and for policy makers to increase funding for food relief. We might pray that those who misuse their power and wealth (including us) be confronted with their evil, repent, and be changed to become generous and humble. We might pray that tyrants will have their hearts broken open by, and for, love. We might pray for healing to be poured out like oil on those who are grieving, or upon fractured relationships. Far beyond simply remembering situations, or crossing our fingers and hoping, we are called to pray for and be *part of* the kingdom's gracious, relational, one-to-one, unpower—the strange victory of love that is unfolding.

In praying for others, we become portals through whom grace can flow, one person at a time. At every moment, people continue to have choice about whether they will be open to this healing energy or not, receiving this love or blocking it, and this is the same for each of us. As we pray for others, often we will not know about, or recognize, the outcomes. That is ok. We are not magicians, God is a not a superhero, and people have agency. We are simply called to play our part in the symphony of grace that is now, and that is unfurling.

In the pages that follow you will find examples of Prayers of Intercession, here called Prayers for the Earth. They seek to express the centrality of being personal and being specific in our praying. This approach to prayer has a great deal in common with

PART THREE: PRAYING IN THE GATHERED COMMUNITY

the Psalms. It is also how Jesus calls people to receive the kingdom, like little children who are frank and persistent (see Matt 7:9–11; Mark 10:13–16; Luke 18:1–8, 15–17).[4] This sample of prayers does not pretend to be comprehensive; clearly not every issue that we could pray for is included. Rather, it is hoped that these offerings spark fresh discussions, and the creation of new prayers in your own faith communities. There are many kinds of communal response for sharing in prayers of intercession. This can include a spoken response, the use of silence, song, or the lighting of candles. There is space to include each of these in the following prayers. Among the spoken responses, the first is inspired by Jesus' prayer of resistance, and I use it often. Each of the responses can be used interchangeably.

---

4. For discussion of Jesus' call to be like a child and how this relates to prayer, see my article "Newborn Infants and Nursing Jesus," 31–41.

Prayers for the Earth

Being of Light, Bread of Life, Breath of Love,
Trinity of Love, we bring our beautiful, broken world to you.

May the worldwide church be known by its love instead of by its judging. Dismantle our pride and divisions, draw us together, and empower us so that we may embody your kindness and joy.

Your kind kingdom come
Your loving will be done

May those who are working for peace and justice in war zones be infused with your wisdom. May those who profit from war be called to account. May those who are disheartened by tragedies be renewed by your presence.

Your kind kingdom come
Your loving will be done

May aid workers and volunteers, here and overseas, be enabled to distribute food to where it is needed. May just tax systems be established so that wealthy elites and global corporations contribute their fair share. Help us to share our resources generously with those in need.

Your kind kingdom come
Your loving will be done

PART THREE: PRAYING IN THE GATHERED COMMUNITY

May the broken hearted and those gripped by depression find shelter under your wings. You who hold every tear we shed, succor the grieving so that they may catch a glimpse of the new life that you long for them.

Your kind kingdom come
Your loving will be done

In the silence, we bring the prayers of our hearts to you:

> *Silence—perhaps with time for spoken prayers, and/or time to light candles*

Your kind kingdom come
Your loving will be done

Together we pray as Jesus taught us—in the version closest to our hearts—the Lord's Prayer

PRAYING FOR OTHERS?

Prayers for the Earth

Most High,
in Jesus you teach us to pray like children,
and so we call on you now, bringing our longings to you.

May justice roll down like waters,
and righteousness like an everlasting stream. (Amos 5:24)

Mother Father God, our creator,
you made all things in your wisdom.
Ignite the hearts of political and corporate leaders so that they prioritize care for the earth

May justice roll down like waters,
and righteousness like an everlasting stream. (Amos 5:24)

May those who misuse their power be brought low.
Feed and satisfy those who thirst for justice
so that all your children may enjoy your gifts.

May justice roll down like waters,
and righteousness like an everlasting stream. (Amos 5:24)

May lasting peace and justice be established in war-torn places: ...
(*these places may be named*)
May stronger policies be created so that the poor and the vulnerable are protected.

May the scourge of human trafficking and exploitation be exposed and stopped.

May justice roll down like waters,
and righteousness like an everlasting stream. (Amos 5:24)

May those who are hurting this day find solace in your tender love.
May the purposeless find their life in you, recognizing and sharing their gifts.
Sustain and challenge us, so that we may be useful in your way of love.

May justice roll down like waters,
and righteousness like an everlasting stream. (Amos 5:24)

And we pray for the worldwide church. Guide leaders, guard those new to Christian faith, may all those who are struggling find wise and loving companions. May your Spirit be poured over your church, illuminating and refining us at this time.

May justice roll down like waters,
and righteousness like an everlasting stream. (Amos 5:24)

And in the silence we bring our prayers to you:

> *Silence—perhaps with time for spoken prayers and/or time to light candles*

We gather these prayer to you, and together pray as Jesus taught us—in the version closest to our hearts—the Lord's Prayer

PRAYING FOR OTHERS?

Prayers for the Earth

Ancient of Days, Wisdom made flesh, Spirit of fire, Triune God, we bring our prayers to you.

Free your world from the power of idols, from fear, and from lies. Empower your church to stand against evil. May we embody the truth that there is enough and joyfully share your news that all are beloved.

> May steadfast love and faithfulness meet
> **May justice and peace kiss each other** (Ps 85:10)

We long for an end to wars. Empower prophets, activists, and artists who expose the truth and call for change. May despots be called to account for their violence. May peace and justice be established in (*space to name particular places*).

> May steadfast love and faithfulness meet
> **May justice and peace kiss each other** (Ps 85:10)

May those who are weeping know your healing presence. May those who hate their work, and those who long for work, receive the support they need. May young and old people be freed from their isolation. May we create pockets of homecoming and grace.

> May steadfast love and faithfulness meet
> **May justice and peace kiss each other** (Ps 85:10)

PART THREE: PRAYING IN THE GATHERED COMMUNITY

In the silence we pray for those on our hearts.

> *Silence—perhaps with time for spoken prayers and/or time to light candles*

May steadfast love and faithfulness meet
May justice and peace kiss each other (Ps 85:10)

We pray through Jesus, and together pray as Jesus taught us—in the version closest to our hearts—the Lord's Prayer.

Prayers for the Earth

May the church in every place be part of the feeding, the clothing, the welcoming and the caring.
May we be ready to be encountered by you in all whom we meet.
May each of us, and the church the world over, be known for our love.

Your kind kingdom come
Your loving will be done

May those working for peace in families, in neighborhoods, and across nations be empowered by your wisdom and creativity, knowing when to speak and when to walk away.
May those who do violence be called to account, face consequences, and be changed.
May those who have been violated know that you grieve with them, and may they experience healing.

Your kind kingdom come
Your loving will be done

May teachers and students be respected and supported in their learning.
May the exhausted taste moments of rest and laughter amidst all that they hold.
May the sick be cared for with kindness, and nurses be strengthened by you.

PART THREE: PRAYING IN THE GATHERED COMMUNITY

May the dying be open to your truth, and their companions know your comfort.

Your kind kingdom come
Your loving will be done

We pray all through Jesus, our liberator and healer, and together we pray as Jesus taught us—in the version closest to our hearts—The Lord's Prayer.

Prayers for the Earth

(Based on Mary's prayer in Luke 1:46–56)

Holy One–Sacred Three,
scatter the proud,
cast down the mighty.

May there be wholeness.
May there be healing.

Lift up the lowly.
Feed the hungry.
Send the rich away to be changed.

May there be wholeness.
May there be healing.

Strengthen the sick.
Gather in the lost.
Dissolve our divisions.

May there be wholeness.
May there be healing.

Embolden all who work for love.
Comfort all who journey through shadowy valleys.

Empower us, and all your church, to participate in your revolution of grace.

May there be wholeness.
May there be healing.

We pray for those on our hearts this day:

> *Silence*

May there be wholeness.
May there be healing.

And together we pray as Jesus taught us—in the version closest to our hearts—The Lord's Prayer.

Prayers for the Earth
Prayer stations

At times we long for quiet, and we struggle to formulate words for the prayers of our hearts. As Paul states, when this happens the Spirit intercedes "with sighs too deep for words" (Rom 8:26). Prayers for the earth can be prayed without using words, either in complete silence or with quiet music in the background. Below is one way of praying together using prayer stations.

Three Prayer Stations are created before worship, one for the world, one for your country, and one for your community. On each of these three tables, placed around the worship space, have a candle and a bowl of sand with tapers to light, or tealight candles laid out around the candle. It is helpful for each table to include a small symbol, or some words, to indicate which station it is. Before beginning this time of prayer, a flame from the Christ candle is lit and carried to each of the three candles (perhaps by children or young people in the community).

With words such as "Let us pray," people are then invited to move between these three stations in their own time. People will return to their seats when they are ready. Some people may choose to remain in their seats and pray, which is fine. This extended time of quiet prayer concludes with the Lord's Prayer.

9

This is my body

HOLDING OUT SOME BREAD at a meal, Jesus says, "Take eat; this is my body" (Matt 26:26; cf. Mark 14:22; Luke 22:19). These are not normal words to say. The strangeness of these words has continued to ricochet through the centuries, offending, shaping, baffling, dividing, and sustaining generations of people. However, due to familiarity with Eucharist liturgies, at times people in the church can miss the shocking nature of what is being said. This is where John's Gospel can help us. While in Mark's, Matthew's, and Luke's Gospels, Jesus first shares these words on the night before he is executed, in John's Gospel Jesus says nothing like this on the night he is betrayed. Instead, Jesus chooses to wash the disciples' feet. After this, Jesus talks at length about love, divine abiding, about the Spirit who is the Advocate, and about being the way, and truth, and life (John 13:1—17:26).

In the delicious and contrary way that John's Gospel unfolds, Jesus talks about being the bread and calls people to eat his own flesh *during* his ministry of healing, forgiving, feeding, and teaching. In this Gospel, Jesus says these strange words after making a feast for the multitudes (John 6:1–15), when the crowds track Jesus down because they long for more (John 6:22–34). In response, Jesus turns and says to them: "I am the bread of life" (John 6:35). Jesus then goes on to assert: "Those who eat my flesh and drink my blood abide in me, and I in them" (John 6:56). This is an invitation to everyone in the crowd to come and be nourished. In John's

Gospel the shocking nature of these words is not glossed over. Readers are bluntly told that it is *because* of these words about eating Jesus' flesh and drinking Jesus' blood, that *many* disciples walk away and are no longer followers (John 6:60–66). Understandably.

In the early Jesus movement the strangeness of this language does not dissipate. As worship practices begin to take shape, sharing bread and wine in Jesus' name is integral, and rumors begin to spread that these Christians are cannibals. We see hints of this accusation already in the rejection of Jesus by swathes of disciples in John's Gospel. When Justin Martyr writes between the 130s and 160s CE, he addresses these accusations (*Dial.* 10). So too does Tertullian, writing a few decades later (*Nat.* 1.7; cf. *Apol.* 7–8). Over the centuries, understandings of Eucharist (literally, meaning thanksgiving) have become entrenched along denominational divides, and in many contexts the wildness of the words has been domesticated. It is also often assumed that the meaning of the language used in Holy Communion is univocal or obvious, even though the words are understood in very different ways in various denominations. This has led to an obscuring of the disruptive and complex beauty at the heart of this feast. In the pages that follow we will seek to reclaim some of the wonder.

As always when engaging with the Bible, attending to context is essential if we seek to truly honor and love our sacred text. When Jesus utters words about bread, wine, and eating his flesh, expressed in different ways across the Gospels, Jesus does so from *within* a particular religious and cultural setting. Jesus' Jewishness is integral to who he is, and to the vast majority of his first followers, and to the first hearers of the Gospels. Across sacred Jewish texts there are rich stories and traditions about bread and wine and nourishment from the Divine. There are the Passover meal traditions, which celebrate God's liberation of the people of Israel from slavery in Egypt (Exod 12:1—13:10). There is manna from heaven that sustains the people while they are wandering in the wilderness (Exod 16:1–36). There is the story of Elisha feeding a crowd of people with barley loaves by God's grace (2 Kgs 4:42–44). There is Woman Wisdom, the female divine, offering her great feast of bread and wine, and her wisdom to all who lack sense (Prov 9:1–6; see also Sir 15:3). In words that the Johannine Jesus echoes, there is Woman Wisdom offering her very self as nourishment to feed from (Sir 24:17–21; see John 6:35). There is the Lord, the shepherd, who sets the table for feasting in the presence of enemies (Ps 23:5). There is the invitation of the Most High in Isaiah, to come and receive wine and milk, even when there is no capacity to pay (Isa 55:1–3). In the concluding chapter of Isaiah, there is the imagery of being breastfed and comforted through God's power (Isa 66:10–13). These rich understandings of the Most High who longs to nourish the people, undergird and infuse Jesus' words about the bread and the wine and his body and blood, and their reception within early Jesus communities, who begin sharing in these worship meals in Jesus' name.

Alongside these understandings, there is also a wider cultural and religious context to consider. While Jewish people, and Jewish Jesus people, believe in one God, this is not the norm in the first century of the Common Era. Within the Greco-Roman world there is widespread belief in the existence of many, many gods and goddesses. The stories of these deities abound, and worship of these deities is commonplace everywhere. This can be hard for those of us who live in monotheistic, or post-monotheistic, cultures to fully appreciate. However, in villages, towns, and cities across the Roman Empire there are temples dedicated to all kinds of gods and goddesses. Often there are several temples, each devoted to a different deity, within one town. The ongoing worship of various gods and goddesses is not confined to public settings, this worship is also important within daily life at home. Rich and poor people have shrines set up to make offerings to their favorite gods or goddesses, whether this be to pay homage to Zeus, Minerva, Apollo, Isis, Poseidon, Venus, or others. Miniature statues of various deities have been recovered from the ruins of homes in the bustling Roman town of Pompeii, preserved for nearly two millennia by the volcanic fallout of the eruption of 79 CE. These household idols give tangible insight into the lived reality of the population—the majority of people—who are living cheek by jowl with these odd, tiny Jesus communities.

Religious worship of various gods and goddesses is commonplace, and expected, in the first century across the quickly expanding Roman Empire. It is the civic duty of people to take food offerings to the local temples in order to please and appease the local gods and goddesses. It is believed (or perhaps at times conveniently asserted) that by fulfilling this duty peace and prosperity could be maintained. Increasingly, in this period, this civic duty is extended to worship of the emperor. This is exemplified by Emperor Augustus (63 BCE–14 CE), named in the infancy narrative of Luke's Gospel (Luke 2:1). During his life Augustus begins claiming to be divine: "the son of god." In the first century, temples are being dedicated to Augustus, and offerings are being made in these temples. While Jewish people are able to gain exemptions from this cultic duty because Judaism is recognized as an old religion by the empire, this is not the case for Christians. Instead, as it becomes clear that this faith is different to Judaism, Jesus followers come under fire.

One of the earliest accusations made against Christians is that they are atheists. This is because they are refusing to participate in worship of these deities, including honoring the emperor, at local temples. In doing so, they are refusing to fulfill their civic duty. Within Justin Martyr's *First Apology*, a text addressed to Emperor Titus, he defiantly responds to this accusation, stating: "Thus we are even called atheists. We do proclaim ourselves atheists as regards those whom you call gods, but not with respect to the Most True God, who is alien to all evil" (Justin, *1 Apol.* 6). Christians are viewed with deep suspicion because of this ongoing civil disobedience. It is feared that as a result of their unwillingness to participate in worshipping the local gods and goddesses, one of these unpredictable deities might unleash punishment upon the towns where people live. Justin ultimately loses his life for his refusal to deny his faith in Christ as the *one* true Lord.

When we recognize this wider cultural context, the shocking texture of Jesus' words begins to solidify. In a context in which people are endlessly told that they must take food offerings to temples to please and appease the pantheon of gods, Jesus, the God One, says the opposite—I want to feed you:

> I am the bread of life. Whoever comes to me will never be hungry and whoever believes in me will never be thirsty.... I am the living bread that came down from heaven. Whoever eats of this bread will live forever, and the bread that I will give for the life of the world is my flesh. (John 6:35, 51)

In Jesus, understandings of power, and in particular divine power, are turned inside out. Here, assumptions about the way the universe works are dismantled. Here, we are confronted with the God who does not require us to bring anything—we do not need to grovel, or perform, or placate. Instead, audaciously, God offers God's very self to us, to quench *our* thirst, and to bring *us* life (John 6:54–55; 7:37–38). This is the mystery at the heart of Eucharist—the explosive provocation that we do not need to appease or impress the Divine. Here, we are confronted with the blunt challenge that all we have to do is gather with empty hands and open hearts and let ourselves be fed.

Those of us living in the consumerist culture of the West may think that we are sophisticated and evolved, no longer afraid of erratic or smiting deities. While we may no longer take offerings to local temples or have shrines set up in our homes to keep the gods or goddesses happy, often we are not far removed from such constructs. We still tend to be bound up in the same kind of transactional thinking. We remain embroiled in lies such as: if we work hard enough, or gain a particular role, or lose weight, or become more popular, or achieve that number of followers—making offerings at the altars of the gods in our culture—then we will be lovable, worthy, find belonging, or be happy. The gods have changed their guise, but our practice of making offerings—working ourselves to death, consuming our way to consolation, or scrolling ourselves into oblivion—remains the same. In Jesus the Christ the illusion is torn asunder. We discover that there are no magic tricks. We are loved without trying. We are lavished by grace in all our brokenness and beauty, longing and hunger, and the invitation of the Divine is to simply and courageously receive:

> Come to me all you that are weary and are carrying heavy burdens, I will give you rest. (Matt 11:28)

In Eucharist, Holy Communion, it is grace *all the way down*. We do not have to bring anything to appease the Most High. Here, Jesus, the face of God among us, longs to feed us. John Knox, with other early Reformers, writes tenderly about this in the *Scots Confession* (1560). Amidst the battles over faith, practice, and ecclesiology, this document proclaims:

> In the Supper, rightly used, Christ Jesus is so joined with us, that he becomes the very nourishment and food for our souls. (*Scots Confession*, ch. 21)

When we put down all the striving and respond to Jesus' call, the lies are undone and the idols are smashed. Being at the table as we are, not as we pretend to be, acknowledging all of our hunger and all of our thirst, without trying to prove our place first, is liberative. Here we are met by the Living One who loves us and who offers the Divine self to nourish us into wholeness.

A note about atonement theology and Eucharist

For people with little connection to the church, and for many within mainstream churches, the Eucharistic language of body and blood causes affront. Just as it was shocking for the disciples surrounding the Johannine Jesus, the language continues to offend. Within contemporary context, offence is not so much linked with concerns about cannibalism, rather the offence stems from the theological framing that commonly accompanies Holy Communion. Within many Eucharistic liturgies across denominations (as well as in hymns and songs), ideas of sacrifice dominate. Jesus is imaged as the lamb who makes the perfect sacrifice, (presumably) for a God who requires this, and we are beneficiaries of this sacrifice. While different versions of this theological framing are common, they are problematic from both theological and biblical perspectives.

From theological perspective, the idea of Jesus being the sacrificial lamb can easily catapult Eucharist practices back into Greco-Roman cultic constructions of worship, in which sacrifice is essential in order to appease the gods. This is despite the reality that Jesus disrupts this entire mechanism. From a biblical perspective there are also concerns. Within John's Gospel, while the author describes John the Baptist seeing Jesus and stating: "Here is the Lamb of God who takes away the sin of the world" (John 1:29), it is less than clear how this is understood within the text. It seems unlikely that the baptizer's imagery of Jesus as the Lamb is linked with understandings of Jesus being a sacrifice. Within Jewish tradition the annual sin offering on the Day of Atonement, is made using goats, not lambs (see Lev 16:1–5). Furthermore, as indicated in the prayers of the Psalms, within Jewish faith it is confidently believed that God can forgive sins, without humans needing to make sin offerings at all (as Ps 51 makes abundantly clear).

A crucial clue for interpreting the Johannine "Lamb of God" language is found in the account of the timing of Jesus' death in this Gospel. Unlike the Synoptic Gospels, in John's Gospel, Jesus' execution occurs on the same day that the Passover lamb is killed. This is clearly significant. Passover is not a feast that is about sin or about the removal of sins. This needs to be underscored because this reality is so often overlooked in the church. Passover, as indicated earlier, is the Jewish feast celebrating God's liberation of the people from slavery in Egypt. Liberation from slavery is the primary metaphor at work within Passover celebrations. Liberation is also integral to John's Gospel.

For the author of John, and for other New Testament authors, the world is not a neutral place. The evil one is present, doing violence and deceiving, as the Johannine Jesus states: "he was a murderer form the beginning" and is "the father of lies" (John 8:44). In direct contrast with the evil one, Jesus is the "way and the truth and the life" (John 14:6)—whose light cannot be overcome (John

1:5). Jesus is the Living One who *liberates* from evil and gathers up all people (John 12:31-32).[1] In John's Gospel, in Jesus the Lamb (John 1:29), the Word (John 1:1), the Bread (John 6:35), the Light (John 8:12), the Vine (John 15:1), the Gate (John 10:9), the Shepherd (John 10:11), and the Resurrection (John 11:25), the path of liberation from evil is embodied. The true Lord and God (John 20:28) does not need or demand sacrifices, but offers God's very self to set us free and nourish us into life.

Within the church various theologies of atonement have developed over time. In recent centuries, this complexity has been flattened out by a singular focus upon understanding Jesus' death as an atoning sacrifice for sin. While such atonement theology—constructed as penal substitution—gives meaning to many, this theological understanding repulses many others. Despite the insistent focus upon this particular construction of theology in Eucharist (and elsewhere) in the church over centuries, followers of Jesus are not given the thin choice between accepting this theology or rejecting the belief that Jesus brings salvation—transformation, healing, and wholeness. John's Gospel makes this clear. Furthermore, when the narratives of the Last Supper across the Synoptic Gospels are attended to, this also becomes apparent. While the language of forgiveness of sins is included in Matthew's account (Matt 26:28), the language of sacrifice is absent from all of the Gospels accounts of the Last Supper, including Matthew's (see Matt 26:26-29; Mark 14:22-25; Luke 22:15-20; see also 1 Cor 11:23-26).[2]

---

1. For further discussion, see Douglas, "Salvation as Liberation."

2. In perhaps the earliest liturgy for Eucharist outside the New Testament, found in The Didache, sin is not the focus of the liturgy, and an institution narrative is not included either (see Did. 9-10). Instead, within this liturgy, there is thanksgiving for Jesus the vine, and child, and for the "spiritual food and drink" of Eucharist. Intriguingly, the references to the bread in this liturgy appear to be linked to accounts of Jesus feeding the multitudes, and thus, this framing may indicate connections with John's Gospel. For further discussion, see Douglas, *Jesus Sophia*, 67-69; Douglas, *Early Church Understandings*, 57-63.

Despite the repetition of particular interpretations of this meal, Eucharist is not intrinsically linked with ideas of sacrifice and atonement theology. Instead, what is central in the New Testament accounts is that Jesus takes up bread and wine, ordinary staples of life, and offers these as somehow bearing divine self-giving to us. In a world that endlessly tells us that there is not enough, and that we are not enough, and that we need to prove our worth, or appease the gods, being confronted by the God who longs to nourish us without us having to do or bring anything first, is groundbreaking. What is, perhaps, even more shocking is that this divine self-giving is not offered to us once. Over and over again Christ calls us to the table to find our place and to be fed. Here we are endlessly freed and remade. This is a gift beyond imagining.

The Eucharist liturgies

Within the Eucharist liturgies offered in the pages that follow, Christ Jesus' nourishment is at the center. Three liturgies are offered, each with a different focus folded around this theme. The first liturgy focuses on the biblical imagery of Jesus as mother. The author of 1 Peter, a letter that may in some way go back to the fallible disciple, encourages diverse Jesus communities to imagine themselves as infants nursing from Jesus the Lord. The author states:

> Like newborn infants, long for the pure, spiritual milk, so that by it you may grow into salvation—if indeed you have tasted that the Lord is good. (1 Pet 2:2–3)

While it has been downplayed for much of the last seventeen hundred years, here the author encourages people to imagine themselves breastfeeding from Jesus, the Lord, who tastes good. I have written at length about this biblical understanding, a significant metaphor in the early church, as reflected in the writings of Clement of Alexandria, as well as in subsequent centuries for theologians such as Julian of Norwich.[3] Rather than rehearsing

---

3. See Douglas, "Newborn Infants and Nursing Jesus," 31–41; Douglas, *Jesus Sophia*, 69–73.

the evidence here, I invite you to dive into these resources. Suffice to say, amidst the ongoing rumors that Jesus communities were partaking in cannibalism, the imagery of breastfeeding from Jesus may have been a more palatable way to proclaim their conviction that in this worship-meal they are being nourished by the risen Jesus.

The focus of the second Eucharist liturgy is Jesus' invitation into life in abundance (John 10:10). This liturgy seeks to disrupt the scarcity narratives and worthiness competitions that our culture endlessly manufactures and consumes, contemporary expressions of cultic worship. The third and final liturgy focuses on the biblical and theological understanding of salvation as liberation. As indicated above, while often ignored, understandings of Jesus' liberation from evil are integral across New Testament texts.

Each of these liturgies intentionally draws from early church understandings, uplifting theological ideas that have been (wilfully or accidently) ignored for centuries. Some actions are offered in italics. Presiders may also like to hold up the bread and wine as expressions of embodied prayer within the institution narrative. It is hoped that these liturgies may offer a path to the table for those who find, or have come to find, the Eucharist alien or offensive. Jesus' wild invitation to come and be fed continues to reverberate throughout creation and is endlessly offered to each one of us.

PART THREE: PRAYING IN THE GATHERED COMMUNITY

Notes on the "Jesus our mother" Eucharist liturgy

This liturgy begins with the first creation account in Genesis 1. It traces God's call to the people of Israel, the gift of the law, and celebrates the incarnation—God coming to us in Jesus. The imagery of Wisdom sweet as honeycomb is found in Sirach (Sir 24:1–22; see also Ps 19:7–10). Language and imagery from John 1:1–18, John 6, and 1 Peter 2:2–3 are integral to this liturgy, as well as John 10:10. This Eucharist prayer also draws from the words of the *Scots Confession* and understandings of the *perichōrēsis*, the Divine Dance of love, within the life of the Triune God (see ch. 2).

Jesus our mother Eucharist liturgy

Invitation

"Like newborn infants long for the pure spiritual milk . . . if indeed you have tasted that the Lord is good." (1 Pet 2:2–3)

Great prayer of thanksgiving

The risen Christ be with you.
And also with you.

Lift up your hearts, and minds, and spirits.
We lift them to the Holy One–Sacred Three.

Let us give thanks to the Triune God.
It is right to give our thanks and praise.

Holy Mystery, Holy Wisdom, Holy Flame,
Blessed Three, Divine Dance of love,
we adore you.

You sang creation into being,
delighting in the goodness of us and the earth,
calling us to join with you in caring for all things.

PART THREE: PRAYING IN THE GATHERED COMMUNITY

When we were lost, you found us,
When we were hungry, you fed us,
When we were warring, you gave us Wisdom, sweet as honeycomb, to guide us.

And when the time was right
you chose to pitch tent among us in person—
Holy Wisdom, your Word, made flesh.

In Jesus you offer life.
In Jesus the kindness of your kingdom is embodied.
In Jesus you bring us home to you, to others, and to ourselves.

In Jesus you offer your very self to us saying:

> Those who eat my flesh and drink my blood
> abide in me and I them. (John 6:56)

Like new born babies we cry out for you.
We are hungry for your sustenance, weary for your embrace;
hold us in your arms and feed us from your very self.

We praise you, Blessed Three, with the faithful of every time and place, joining with the choirs of angels and the whole of creation in the eternal hymn:

> **Holy, holy, holy One,**
> **Source of power, tenderness, and delight,**
> **heaven and earth are full of your glory.**
> **Hosanna in the highest.**
>
> **Blessed is the One who comes in the name of the Lord.**
> **Hosanna in the highest.**
>
> *Invite the congregation to stand, if not already standing*

THIS IS MY BODY

Blessed is Jesus, Wisdom embodied,
who made feasts out of scraps
and who gathers us now to be nourished.

On the night before Jesus died,
on the evening of devastating betrayal,
Jesus took a loaf of bread, blessed it, and broke it, saying:

> This is my body, which is for you.
> Do this in remembrance of me.

In the same way, also the cup, after supper saying;

> This cup is the new covenant in my blood.
> Do this whenever you drink it in remembrance of me

As we eat this bread and drink this cup
we are fed by Jesus our mother—
and we testify to the unfolding of God's new creation
in and through the disruptive living, dying, rising, and ongoing presence of Jesus
among us in healing love—now, and in the culmination of all things.

> *With the presider, the people are invited to raise their hands*

Holy Flame, Great Spirit, you labor throughout creation birthing new life,
lavish these gifts and our very beings with your grace,
that Christ Jesus may be the very nourishment and food for our souls.

All glory be to you, Blessed Trinity,
Holy Mystery, Holy Wisdom, Holy Flame,
as it was in the beginning, is now, and ever shall be. Amen.

PART THREE: PRAYING IN THE GATHERED COMMUNITY

The Lord's Prayer

In the version closest to our hearts

Receiving the elements

Holding the elements out to the congregation

Jesus says: "I am the living bread that came down from heaven." (John 6:51)
Jesus says: "Let anyone who is thirsty come to me." (John 7:37)

Friends, the Source of all longs to feed us.
You are known by name and you are loved.

Distribution

> Jesus, the bread of life, given for you.
> Jesus, the true vine, poured out for you.

After receiving

Blessed Three, Holy Mystery, Holy Wisdom, Holy Flame,
we are your beloved children.
You have nourished us with your very self and we adore you.

Continue to abide in us, as we abide in you,
so that in our words, our actions, and our being, your love flows through us, sharing the taste of your grace wherever we go.

Through Jesus our sustainer we pray. Amen.

Notes on the "I will give you rest" Eucharist liturgy

This liturgy draws from understandings within Matthew's Gospel. Here Jesus is Emmanuel, God-with-us (Matt 1:23). In this Gospel, speaking as Sophia, Jesus offers rest to all those who are exhausted and carry heavy burdens (Matt 11:28), without any caveats about being "worthy" or earning our place. Words from the Nicene Creed and Micah (Micah 6:8) are incorporated into this liturgy, as well as the promise of the reconciliation of all things, found in the Colossians hymn (Col 1:20).

PART THREE: PRAYING IN THE GATHERED COMMUNITY

I will give you rest
Eucharist liturgy

Invitation

While tyrants demand tributes and the world tell us that we are never enough, Jesus says, "Come to me, all you that are weary and carrying heavy burdens, and I will give you rest." (Matt 11:28)

Let us gather to Jesus Emmanuel, God-with-us, Light from Light, true God from true God.

Great thanksgiving prayer

Jesus Emmanuel be with you.
And also with you.

Lift up your hearts.
We lift them to the Lord.

Let us give thanks to the servant Lord our God.
It is right to give our thanks and praise.

Holy One–Sacred Three,
Ground of our being, Water of life, Fire of truth,
we worship you, offering our thanks and praise.

THIS IS MY BODY

You fashion all things.
You care for each one.
You declare the goodness of the earth.

You call humanity,
—made in your image, made for community—
to care for creation, as you do.

You called a people to be a light to the nations,
doing justice, loving kindness, and walking humbly with you.
You continue to shower mercy.

And when the time was right,
in order to reconcile all things,
your love became personal, your Word—your Story—made flesh.

In Jesus' feeding, forgiving, and befriending
we encounter your relentless grace.

In Jesus' teaching and doing compassion
our fear is dissolved.

In Jesus' living, dying, and rising
we are confronted with your love more powerful than hate, and
death.

As Great Spirit once breathed over the waters
she continues to work throughout creation,
disrupting empires, birthing the new, and weaving the love.

And so we praise you with the faithful of every time and place,
joining with the choirs of angels and the whole of creation,
in the eternal hymn:

PART THREE: PRAYING IN THE GATHERED COMMUNITY

Sung or spoken

Holy, holy, holy, Lord,
God of power and might,
heaven and earth are full of your glory.
Hosanna in the highest.

Blessed is the One who comes in the name of the Lord.
Hosanna in the highest.

Invite people to stand, if they are not standing already

Blessed is Jesus, God-with-us,
who feasted with friends and failures, with outcasts and searchers,
and who now shares this meal in our midst.

On the night before Jesus died,
on the evening of betrayal,
Jesus took a loaf of bread, broke it, and blessed it saying:

> This is my body, which is for you.
> Do this in remembrance of me.

In the same way, also the cup, after supper saying:

> This cup is the new covenant in my blood.
> Do this whenever you drink it in remembrance of me.

As we eat this bread and drink this cup,
we testify to the unfolding of God's new creation—
in and through the life, death, and resurrection of Jesus, the Anointed One,
and in the completion of all things when the kin(g)dom comes in disruptive glory.

With the presider, the people are invited to raise their hands

Spirit Holy, as we gather with empty hands and open hearts,
enliven these humble gifts of the earth, this bread and this wine,
and saturate us with your grace, that we may receive your life
within and among us.

As we remember Jesus' self-giving, may we be re-membered;
as we enter this story, may we be restored and re-storied;
and so take up our part in your drama of love for all things.

All glory be to you, Holy One–Sacred Three,
Ground of our being, Water of life, Fire of truth,
As it was in the beginning, is now, and ever shall be. Amen.

The Lord's Prayer

In the version closest to our hearts

Receiving the elements

Holding the elements out to the congregation

Jesus says, "I am the bread of life whoever comes to me will never be hungry." (John 6:35)
Jesus says, "I am the true vine abide in me as I abide in you." (John 15:1, 3)

May we who share these gifts be found in Christ
and Christ found in us.

Distribution

> Christ, the bread of life, given for you.
> Christ, the true vine, poured out for you.

Prayer after receiving

Jesus, God-with-us, our homecoming,
we praise you for feeding us and giving us rest.
Lead us forward now in the power of Spirit Holy,
that we may savor your joy, embody your kindness, and whisper your hope wherever we go.
To you be the glory.
May it be so.
Amen.

Notes on the "Jesus our liberator" Eucharist liturgy

Particularly in Mark's Gospel and in John's Gospel, Jesus' salvation is linked to understandings of liberation. Here, as in many places in the New Testament, this liberation is understood to be from cosmic evil. As discussed above, in John's Gospel Jesus embodies the truth and life that stand in direct contrast with the lies and violence of the evil one (see John 8:44–45; 12:31–32; 14:6). In Mark's Gospel the language of ransom is used to give expression to this understanding of liberation. Elsewhere, this imagery, and the imagery of rescue are utilized (Mark 10:45; see also Col 1:13, 20; 1 Tim 2:6; Rev 1:17–18). This thanksgiving prayer draws from this rich seam of early church theology.

PART THREE: PRAYING IN THE GATHERED COMMUNITY

Jesus our liberator
Eucharist liturgy

Invitation

Friends, Christ is the light of the world—
the light that the darkness could not overcome.
Christ is our freedom and our food—and this is Christ's table.
Come, all is prepared.

Great thanksgiving prayer

The risen Christ be with you.
And also with you.

Lift up your hearts and minds and spirits.
We lift them to the Holy One–Sacred Three.

Let us give thanks to the Triune God.
It is right to give our thanks and praise.

Almighty, All-tender God,
our beginning and our ending,
you love us into being,
creating, liberating, and blessing us.

When we were pinned down by deception,
when we were drowning in fear,
when we were fuelled by hostility,
when we were far off from you,
you walked towards us in Jesus, the Christ,
the fullness of your power disclosed in person,
your way, your truth, your life enfleshed—
love stronger than evil,
love mightier than death.
In Jesus the lies of violence are undone.
In Jesus we are rescued from hate and dread.
In Jesus we are reclaimed for life.

Almighty, All-tender God,
Holy One–Sacred Three,
we bless you for coming to us in Jesus—
our Ransom, our Rescuer, our Reconciler.

We praise you with the faithful of every time and place,
joining with the choirs of angels and the whole of creation,
in the eternal hymn:

Sung or spoken

Holy, holy, holy, Lord,
God of power and might,
heaven and earth are full of your glory.
Hosanna in the highest.

Blessed is the One who comes in the name of the Lord.
Hosanna in the highest.

Invite people to stand, if they are not standing already

PART THREE: PRAYING IN THE GATHERED COMMUNITY

Blessed is Jesus, our freedom and food,
who offers this meal in our midst.

On the night before Jesus died,
on the evening of his betrayal,
Jesus took a loaf of bread, broke it, and blessed it saying:

> This is my body, which is for you.
> Do this in remembrance of me.

In the same way, also the cup, after supper, saying:

> This cup is the new covenant in my blood.
> Do this whenever you drink it in remembrance of me.

As we eat this bread and drink this cup,
we testify to the unfurling kingdom—the fierce kindness of God
in and through the life, and death, and resurrection of Jesus,
and in the liberation of all things when Christ Jesus comes again.

> *With the presider, the people are invited to raise their hands*

Great Spirit, infuse this bread and this wine and we who gather—
that we may receive your life to our life
and taste the joy of your salvation.
Through Jesus we pray. Amen.

The Lord's Prayer

> *In the version closest to our hearts*

The breaking of the bread

Holding the elements out to the congregation

The Bread of life given for you.
The cup of liberation poured out for you.
The gifts of God for the people of God.

Distribution

> The body of Christ given for you.
> The blood of Christ poured out for you.

After receiving

Almighty, All-tender God,
thank you for the wonder of the truth—
> that there is enough,
> that we are enough,
> and that we have a place at the table.

You free us and you feed us, we adore you.
May we exude your light, embody your love, and share the scent of your hope wherever we go.
Through Jesus our liberator we pray. Amen.

Conclusion

10

Homeward Bound

TWICE, IN THE LAST two weeks of writing this book, in two different congregations, in two different worship settings, with two different people each reading a different psalm, the person has had to pause mid-sentence. Upon each occasion, the reader was literally moved to tears by the ancient prayer that they were giving voice to. The psalm was naming something deep within their own lives in that moment, and their emotions spilled over. In the stilting voice, and the unexpected silence, with people looking up wondering what was happening, the power of the psalm was magnified. While these readers may (or may not) have felt embarrassment about their vulnerability, it was an extraordinary gift to receive. The distance between the composition of these words millennia ago and our own lives was collapsed in an instant.

This is the power of prayer. This book has traced the reality that beyond the stereotypes of prayer as magical thinking, reciting words, or a task required to fulfill the obligations of faithfulness (in order to please or convince an unpredictable God), prayer is about letting our deepest, clunkiest selves be open to the Living One who longs to meet us as we are. We long for the living waters, as the psalmist proclaims (Ps 42:1). We long to be ourselves and find our true home and be nourished by the real—to finally breathe out and relax—knowing that we are loved and belong within our own skin, within our relationships, upon this good earth, and within the embrace of the One who is beyond our imagining. For Christians,

CONCLUSION

prayer is about authentic openness, wrestling, and being with this One, the expansive Loving One, who chooses to make camp with us in Jesus, and abide within us in Spirit Holy. This is our homecoming. There are no tricks, no shortcuts, no easy fixes, and no competitions.

As *Rewilding Prayer* explores, homecoming is not static. Nor is it linear. The spiritual life is a wild journey of getting real, getting lost, and getting real again. Inconveniently, it does not move from one easily ascended level to another and there are no gold stamps for achievement along the way. To be open to this kind of homecoming will be hard and unpredictable. There will be times of desolation and consolation, wilderness and feast. If we seek to remain open we will be confronted with ugly truths about ourselves, others, and about our simplistic understandings of God. Life will be undone, and it will be liberation. We will be changed and remade through the Spirit's grace, and we will slowly, slowly, become more like Jesus, the face of God among us.

As the worldwide church wrestles with its place in our rapidly changing global village we need to stop panicking and, instead, be open to the demanding gift that this season offers. Now is the time for us to do the work of becoming clear about what is important to maintain if we are to be faithful to Jesus and what is cultural habit that needs to be jettisoned. It will be costly for there is much in the church's life that needs to be discarded: from the idol of pretending that God is a man, to the church as social club, to pretending that buildings are essential, or that Christian faith is easy, or makes life successful. As we do this work of decluttering, cultivating communities of authentic pray-ers will be essential. Indeed, this may be the greatest priority that we are called to.

At this time, supporting people to move beyond the simplicity of fairytale (or nightmare) images of God is essential. Supporting people to put down notions of prayer as the recitation of words—whether empty praise or shopping lists of doom—is essential. Supporting people to learn to shut up and listen for the Divine who is moving with healing in her wings is essential, both in our communal worship and in our personal lives. We need to stop insulting people with the superficial, and instead throw open the gates so that people are able to enter into the rugged complexity of their own lives, theology, the biblical text, and being with the Divine. This book seeks to offer a little of this, the raw beauty that awaits us.

CONCLUSION

Notes on A Simple Midweek Service

In the final pages of this book, you will find one last liturgy. It was originally composed for the Richmond Uniting Church congregation to use online for a midweek service during the very long COVID lockdowns in Melbourne (some of the longest lockdowns in the world). Uniting Church congregations in various places have used it since. You will see themes and language introduced throughout *Rewilding Prayer* woven into this liturgy, as well as imagery from a Celtic prayer about kindling love for friend and foe.[1] The liturgy works well online as it holds space for written prayers, spontaneous prayer, Bible readings, and shared silence. It can be led by anyone. The readings from the Psalm and the Gospel might be from the lectionary for the following Sunday.

Since writing this liturgy, I have discovered that it also works well in-person, with large or small groups. For families or friends worshipping together at home it can offer a simple structure that genuinely includes children, and people of various abilities. For those who long to share in worship at home, but feel awkward about how to do this, this liturgy might be a useful resource. Over time people become confident in participating in the shared responses, and in sharing aloud their own prayers of thanks and their prayers for others, often with unadorned confidence. Crucially, this liturgy also offers a tangible way of stepping into the currents of silence together. When using this liturgy in person, and particularly with children, it can be good to offer space for briefly sharing thoughts about the readings *after* the shared silence. The Bible references within the liturgy are retained so that it can be easily shared with others who may not have read the whole book (yet). The service usually goes for around twenty-five minutes.

I offer the final blessing of this liturgy for you.

1. See the prayer "Blessing of the kindling" I, 23, in De Waal, *Celtic Vision*, 74.

A Simple Midweek Service

Opening Prayer

We greet you, Holy One–Sacred Three,
Holy Mystery, Holy Wisdom, Holy Flame.

Ancient of Days (Dan 7:9, 11, 22),
Ground of our being:
We praise you.

Jesus, bright Morning Star (2 Pet 1:19),
Hope of our hearts:
We praise you.

Spirit Holy, Advocate and truth (John 14:16–17, 21–21),
Birther of love:
We praise you.

Prayers of Gratitude and praise

Blessed Trinity,
we praise you for coming among us in Jesus:
healing, teaching, and feasting
in friendship and fierce compassion;
dying, rising, and abiding with us now
in friendship and fierce compassion.
We praise you for coming to us in Spirit Holy:

drawing us ever closer to truth and grace,
burning away the fear,
setting us free for love.
We praise you with all of creation.

> *We share our thanks for the times we have experienced love or witnessed beauty, responding after each prayer:*
> Amen
> **We praise you**

Readings from Sacred Scripture

> Psalm
> Gospel

For these words of faith and Jesus the Word
Thanks be to God.

> *Five-minute shared silence after the readings*

Prayers for the earth

You call us into your love for all things,
and so we pray for our beautiful, broken world.
Kindle within us a flame of love:
for kindred, for friend, and for foe
for stranger, for neighbor, and for ourselves.

> *Moment of stillness*

We pray for those people and places on our hearts.
May there be healing and hope, kindness and justice.

We name those people and places, responding after each prayer:
    May your kind kingdom come
    May your loving will be done

Together let us pray as Jesus taught us:

The Lord's Prayer in the version closest to our hearts

Blessing

Let us bless ourselves, and one another, with the blessing of God:

May the Blessed Trinity be with us all,
may the Source of all be upholding you,
may radiant Christ be infusing you,
may Spirit Holy be encircling you,
every step that you take in this stormy world.
In the name of Christ.
Amen.

Bibliography

Augustine. *Confessions: A New Translation by Henry Chadwick*. Oxford World's Classics. Oxford: Oxford University Press, 2008.
———. *On Christian Doctrine*. Translated by J. F. Shaw. The Works of Aurelius Augustine, Bishop of Hippo 9. Edinburgh: T&T Clark, 1873.
The Basis of Union. Uniting Church in Australia, 1992.
Calvin, John. *The Institutes of Christian Religion*. Edited by John T. McNeill. Translated by Ford Lewis Battles. Louisville: Westminster John Knox Press, 2006.
Champion, Denise. *Yarta Wandatha*. Adelaide: Champion, 2014.
Clement of Alexandria. *Christ the Educator*. Translated by Simon P. Wood. The Fathers of the Church 23. Washington, DC: The Catholic University Press, 1954.
Cotter, Jim. *Prayer at Night's Approaching*. New York: Morehouse, 1997.
De Waal, Esther, ed. *The Celtic Vision: Prayers and Blessings from the Outer Hebrides*. London: Darton, Longman, and Todd, 1988.
Douglas, Sally. *The Church ~~Triumphant~~ as Salt: Becoming the Community Jesus Speaks About*. Melbourne: Coventry, 2021.
———. *Early Church Understandings of the Female Divine: The Scandal of the Scandal of Particularity*. LNTS 557. London: Bloomsbury T&T Clark, 2016.
———. "Jesus' Impact on Understandings of Gender: Attending to First Century Dialogue." In *The Impact of Jesus of Nazareth: Historical, Theological and Pastoral Perspectives*, edited by Peter G. Bolt and James R. Harrison, 155–78. Social and Pastoral Studies 2. Sydney: Sydney College of Divinity, 2021.
———. *Jesus Sophia: Returning to Woman Wisdom in the Bible, Practice, and Prayer*. Eugene, OR: Cascade, 2023.
———. "Newborn Infants and Nursing Jesus (1 Pet 2:2–3): The Petrine Metaphor's Disruption of Androcentric Renderings of God and the Child." *Biblical Theology Bulletin* 53 (2023) 31–41.

BIBLIOGRAPHY

———. "The Problem with Powerlessness: Attending to Power and Authority in Matthew's Wisdom Christology." In *Contemporary Feminist Theologies: Power, Authority, Love*, edited by Kerrie Handasyde et al., 59–71. London: Routledge, 2021.

———. "Salvation as Liberation: (Re)Imagining Salvation." *Uniting Church Studies* 1 (2025) 7–17.

Haidt, Jonathan. *The Anxious Generation: How the Great Rewiring of Childhood Is Causing an Epidemic of Mental Illness.* New York: Penguin, 2024.

Hall, Judith. *In Their Midst: Worshipping with Children.* Melbourne: Broughton, 2011.

Hansen, Michael. *The Gospels for Prayer.* Notre Dame: Ave Maria, 2003.

Henderson-Espinoza, Robyn. *Activist Theology.* Minneapolis: Fortress, 2019.

Johnson, Elizabeth. *She Who Is: The Mystery of God in Feminist Theological Discourse.* New York: Crossroad, 2005.

Julian of Norwich. *Revelations of Divine Love, Long Text.* Translated by Elizabeth Spearing. London: Penguin, 1998.

Justin Martyr. *The First Apology, The Second Apology, Dialogue with Trypho Exhortation to the Greeks, Discourse to the Greeks, The Monarchy of the Rule of God.* Translated by Thomas B. Falls. The Fathers of the Church 6. Washington, DC: The Catholic University of America Press, 2008.

LaCugna, Catherine Mowry. *God for Us: The Trinity and Christian Life.* New York: HarperCollins, 1991.

Miriam-Rose Foundation. "Dadirri: The Quiet Stillness Inside Us." https://www.miriamrosefoundation.org.au/dadirri/.

O'Donohue, John. *To Bless This Space Between Us: A Book of Blessings.* New York: Convergent, 2008.

Schüssler Fiorenza, Elizabeth. *Jesus: Miriam's Child, Sophia's Prophet. Critical Issues in Feminist Christology.* London: SCM, 1995.

Scots Confession. Edinburgh: Scottish Parliament, 1560.

Taylor, W. David. *Open and Unafraid: The Psalms as a Guide to Life.* Nashville: Nelson, 2020.

Uniting in Worship 2. Sydney: Uniting Church Press, 2010.

Wesley, John. "The Plain Account of Genuine Christianity." In *John and Charles Wesley: Selected Prayers, Hymns, Journal Notes, Sermons, Letters, and Treatises,* edited by Frank Whaling, 121–33. Classics of Western Spirituality. London: SPCK, 1981.

Westminster Shorter Catechism. London, 1648.

www.ingramcontent.com/pod-product-compliance
Lightning Source LLC
Chambersburg PA
CBHW031817220426
43662CB00007B/685

"There is deep pastoral and biblical wisdom in these honest, unfussy prayers and reflections. Accept Douglas's invitation to plunge into prayer anew!"

—**Amy Plantinga Pauw**, Henry P. Mobley Professor of Doctrinal Theology, Louisville Presbyterian Seminary, USA

"In *Rewilding Prayer*, Sally Douglas weaves theological reflection with practical resources: blessings, liturgies, and daily prayers designed to anchor the spiritual life in honesty, silence, and community. It is both a critique of how prayer has been tamed by habit and hierarchy, and a gentle yet insistent call to rediscover prayer as wild encounter with the divine."

—**Tim Nash**, Founder, *Nomad Podcast*

"Sally Douglas teaches us that prayer is a 'call to the real.' With passion and honesty, she invites us to 'live close to the fire' of liberating divine grace. She challenges us to shake off habits of rote words and exclusively male imagery for God. Her prayers and liturgies are deeply scriptural and wildly poetic. These are living springs, to which I will return again and again."

—**Steven Shakespeare**, Professor of Continental Philosophy of Religion, Liverpool Hope University, United Kingdom

"*Rewilding Prayer* invites the reader into a deep and honest conversation about our understanding of prayer. Encouraging us to be authentic, embedded in Scripture, and theologically engaged, Douglas brings to the fore the important questions of how and why we pray. *Rewilding Prayer* offers fresh language, gentle promptings, and ways to embody prayer individually and in community. More than a book about prayer—Douglas has gifted us a challenge, an invitation, a treasury."

—CATHIE LAMBERT, Director of Pastoral Theology and Ministry Studies, Uniting College for Leadership and Theology, Adelaide, Australia

"*Rewilding Prayer* is a gift and rich resource! Sally Douglas inspires us to pray with 'guts and integrity amidst the chaos' of everyday life. The book is a wonderful blend of theology, praxis, and personal experience. Indeed, a rich resource that inspires prayer and brings us back to the heart of praying to a 'God beyond gender' and to 'faith beyond formulas.'"

—SEFOROSA CARROLL, Acting Principal, United Theological College, Charles Stuart University, Australia

"In *Rewilding Prayer*, Sally Douglas turns the eyes of prayer to the world. Here are prayers for insomnia, tea breaks, confession, change and receiving terrible news. Sally's vast intellect—linguistic, theological, secular, prayerful—is attuned to human experience, and concerned with shaping language that is sensitive, straightforward, devout, and daring."

—PÁDRAIG Ó TUAMA, Host, *Poetry Unbound*